History of Naval Warfare

A Captivating Guide to the Strategies, Battles, and Innovations That Have Shaped Maritime History

© Copyright 2025 - All rights reserved.

The content contained within this book may not be reproduced, duplicated, or transmitted without direct written permission from the author or the publisher.

Under no circumstances will any blame or legal responsibility be held against the publisher, or author, for any damages, reparation, or monetary loss due to the information contained within this book, either directly or indirectly.

Legal Notice:

This book is copyright protected. It is only for personal use. You cannot amend, distribute, sell, use, quote, or paraphrase any part, or the content within this book, without the consent of the author or publisher.

Disclaimer Notice:

Please note the information contained within this document is for educational and entertainment purposes only. All effort has been executed to present accurate, up-to-date, reliable, and complete information. No warranties of any kind are declared or implied. Readers acknowledge that the author is not engaging in the rendering of legal, financial, medical, or professional advice. The content within this book has been derived from various sources. Please consult a licensed professional before attempting any techniques outlined in this book.

By reading this document, the reader agrees that under no circumstances is the author responsible for any losses, direct or indirect, that are incurred as a result of the use of the information contained within this document, including, but not limited to, errors, omissions, or inaccuracies.

Free Bonus from Captivating History (Available for a Limited time)

Hi History Lovers!

Now you have a chance to join our exclusive history list so you can get your first history ebook for free as well as discounts and a potential to get more history books for free!

Simply visit the link below to join.

Or, Scan the QR code!

captivatinghistory.com/ebook

Also, make sure to follow us on Facebook, X, and YouTube by searching for Captivating History.

Table of Contents

INTRODUCTION 1
CHAPTER 1 - THE DAWN OF NAVAL WARFARE 3
CHAPTER 2 - TRIREMES AND TYRANTS 9
CHAPTER 3 - THE ROMAN NAVAL DOMINANCE 17
CHAPTER 4 - THE VIKING LONGSHIPS 27
CHAPTER 5 - THE AGE OF EXPLORATION AND NAVAL EXPANSION 34
CHAPTER 6 - THE LINE OF BATTLE AND NAVAL TACTICS 44
CHAPTER 7 - THE IRONCLADS AND THE INDUSTRIAL REVOLUTION 53
CHAPTER 8 - THE WORLD WARS AND NAVAL WARFARE 60
CHAPTER 9 - THE COLD WAR AND NUCLEAR NAVIES 74
CHAPTER 10 - MODERN NAVAL CONFLICTS AND TECHNOLOGIES 79
CONCLUSION 86
HERE'S ANOTHER BOOK BY CAPTIVATING HISTORY THAT YOU MIGHT LIKE 89
FREE BONUS FROM CAPTIVATING HISTORY (AVAILABLE FOR A LIMITED TIME) 90
REFERENCES 91
IMAGE SOURCES 100

Introduction

Human history is extensive, and much has happened. However, there are few elements that have shaped the destiny of nations as profoundly as naval warfare. From the windswept decks of ancient triremes to the steel hulls of modern battleships, the quest for maritime dominance has been a large driver of innovation, exploration, and conflict. In this book, we'll take you on a voyage through time to explore the fascinating evolution of naval warfare and its indelible impact on the world we know today.

The sea has always drawn human attention. It is still viewed as a realm of vast opportunities and formidable challenges. Our interaction with the sea is full of stories of humanity's ingenuity and bravery, of our ancestors' towering ambition and sometimes their tragic overreach. As we explore naval history, we will uncover the stories of civilizations that rose and fell almost by the power of their fleets alone. You'll discover tales of epic battles that decided the fate of empires and the relentless pursuit of technological advancements that would turn the tide of wars.

We're going to begin in the mist-shrouded rivers and seas of ancient times when the first sailors ventured into this unexplored territory. We will explore how the Egyptians, Greeks, Romans, and Vikings each contributed to the early chapters of naval history, not just because of their conquests but also because of the advancements they made in shipbuilding, navigation, and maritime strategy.

As we continue forward in time, we'll see the transformative power of naval warfare and how it shaped the modern world. The Age of

Exploration opened new frontiers that were driven by the twin engines of curiosity and conquest. The battle tactics of the 17th and 18th centuries, the steel-clad leviathans of the Industrial Revolution, and the silent predators of the world's oceans in the 20th century all marked new eras in naval warfare and the changing dynamics of power, technology, and geopolitics.

As we move into the 21st century, we'll find ourselves in a world where the challenges and the stakes of maritime dominance are as high as they ever have been. The seas will always remain the domain of strategic importance and a theater for demonstrating power, securing trade routes, and, interestingly, addressing global challenges like piracy and environmental disasters.

History of Naval Warfare is written for the curious mind. It's a guide for those who want to understand not just the how and the what but also the why of naval history. This is a story of human endeavor, a story of the restless spirit that drives us to explore beyond the next wave and to build ships that reach for the horizon. These are stories of the people who wanted to write their names not only on the sea but also in the annals of history.

Chapter 1 – The Dawn of Naval Warfare

Humanity's obsession with the sea dates back thousands of years. There is evidence of seafaring and trade between civilizations in ancient times. The earliest maritime endeavors were characterized by the development of the first prehistoric boats, which are said to have been created as early as fifty-five thousand years ago. As far as we can tell, these were simple dugout canoes used by various Stone Age populations.

The Austronesian peoples, in particular, were thought to be pioneers when it came to ocean-going boat technology. They utilized multihulls, outriggers, crab claw sails, and tanja sails to rapidly expand into the Indian and Pacific Oceans. Their early voyages were driven by a mix of curiosity and survival, and they laid the foundations for future maritime explorations and even cultural exchange. Their knowledge of the ocean, which they gained from experience and then passed down through the generations, was crucial for navigating and surviving the treacherous waters. They reached distant lands like New Guinea and the Solomon Islands.

These early maritime innovations laid the groundwork for significant trade routes in later history, including the maritime Silk Road that connected South Asia and the Arabian Sea by around 1000 to 600 BCE.

The Naval Power of Ancient Egypt

One of the first great civilizations that used ships for more than just travel and trade was the ancient Egyptians. The Egyptian navy has a storied history that reflects Egypt's strategic and economic interests, which started in the very early periods of the state's formation along the Nile. Their navy played a vital role in their defense and in expanding Egyptian trade networks and asserting power across the Mediterranean and beyond.

From very early on, Egypt relied on its navy for wartime activities and peaceful trade. The earliest Egyptian ships date to around 3000 BCE, as we can see depicted on the Gebel el-Arak knife. On one side of the hippopotamus tusk handle is a battle scene showing Egyptians defending themselves against another force.

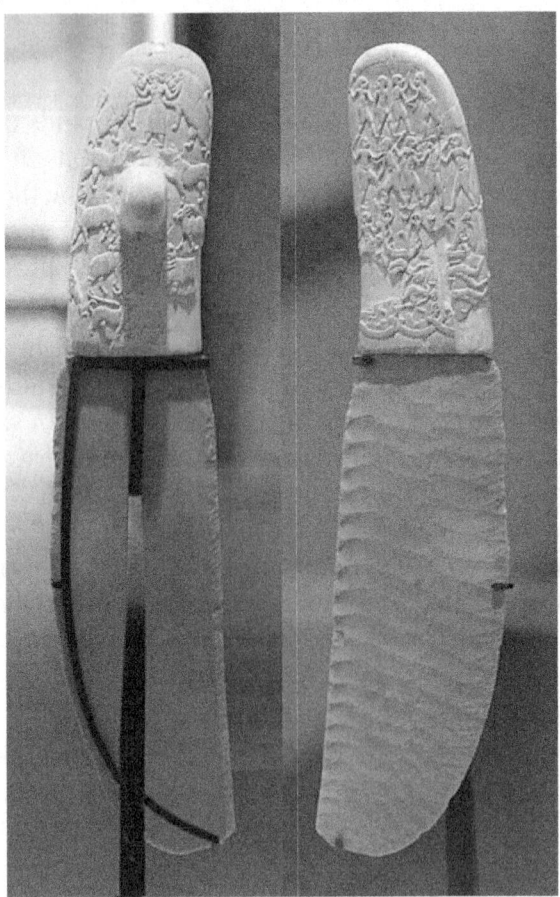

The Gebel el-Arak knife. [1]

These early ships were some of the oldest planked boats discovered. They allowed the Egyptians to control the Nile Valley and were also closely connected to Egyptian ritual preparations for the afterlife since some were found buried near tombs and monuments. Pharaoh Sahure (r. c. 2487-2475 BCE) expanded Egypt's overseas trade well into the Mediterranean and Red Sea. They even reached as far as Southeast Asia and traded for goods like cedar from Lebanon and incense from Punt.

One of the first well-documented moments of naval warfare was the battle against the Sea Peoples during the reign of Ramesses III (r. c. 1186-1155 BCE). The Egyptian navy and its capabilities were a huge part of the Egyptians' ability to repel the invaders who threatened the Nile Delta. Their fleet consisted of warships, galleys, and light craft, which successfully repulsed the Sea Peoples. The Sea Peoples had already destroyed the Hittites and other major cities in the area. Egypt's wealth was well known, and they knew the Sea Peoples would travel up the Nile next.

This naval battle is accounted on the temple relief of Medinet Habu, which states, "I prepared the river mouth like a strong wall with warships, galleys, and light craft. They were completely equipped both fore and aft with brave fighters carrying their weapons, and infantry of all the pick of Egypt, like lions roaring upon the mountain tops."[i]

Ramesses did take the battle to the Sea Peoples on land first. It was said he dreamed that he saw Ptah handing him a sword and telling him to be brave and attack his enemies. He was successful on land, protecting Egypt's easternmost border. After this land battle, Ramesses returned to Egypt, where his naval preparations had already been completed in his absence. It was said that he coaxed the Sea Peoples into the mouth of the Nile, where his naval fleet had prepared an ambush. Hundreds of archers hid in the papyrus reed beds. Once the Sea Peoples' ships had started traveling down the Nile, his archers took fire. They kept up a continuous volley of thousands of arrows and drove the enemy's ships right into his own Egyptian fleet, which had cut off their escape route. The Sea Peoples were utterly defeated.

Egyptian Ship Design

As with any ship, how far they can travel in a day is really dependent on conditions. On average, ancient Egyptian vessels were able to travel

---

[i] Shaw, Ian (1999). *Egyptian Warfare and Weapons.* Shire Publications.

around eighty kilometers a day. Each ship averaged about seventy-five feet long and carried a week's worth of supplies and twenty to fifty men.

Egyptian ships didn't use a keel like on later wooden ships. Instead, a rope was pulled tightly from bow to stern to strengthen the structure. Later, the Egyptians replaced this with a central gangway. This wasn't just a form of strengthening and stabilizing the boats; it was also used as a platform for archers. Unlike the early Viking ships, there were no wooden pegs holding the boards together. The ancient Egyptians didn't even use nails. These boats were bound with rope. They held a singular mast that held a square sail. Each boat could have up to twenty oars to propel it and two large rudders that could be operated separately.

Despite their seemingly rudimentary design, the largest Egyptian vessels weighed around eighty tons, which isn't that much smaller than the ships we're used to and associate with Columbus and later European explorers.

The Minoan Navy

The Minoan civilization flourished from about 3000 to 1100 BCE. They were centered on the island of Crete and are known as the earliest civilization in Europe. As a Bronze Age civilization, the Minoans left a significant mark with their monumental architecture, elaborate seals, pottery, figurines, and vibrant and colorful frescoes that decorated the walls of their palaces, such as that at Knossos and Phaistos.

The Minoan society was complex and highly advanced. They had extensive trade networks that reached well beyond Crete into the Aegean Sea and the eastern Mediterranean. They were particularly well known for their advanced ship construction techniques and maritime skills. They established themselves as a dominant sea power in the ancient world.

The Minoans used celestial navigation techniques similar to those known by the Polynesians despite the fact they lived more than tens of thousands of miles apart, not to mention thousands of years. The Minoans craved access to gold, ivory, and tin, and in order to get them, they had to possess advanced sailing techniques.

King Minos is thought to have had the world's first professional navy, which was as legendary as he was. Much of what we know about the Minoan navy comes from the legendary tales of King Minos. His stories are intertwined with the mythology and history of ancient Crete and the Minoan civilization. King Minos and his feats are often associated with the Minoan civilization's peak. Greek mythology and later historians agree that King Minos ruled Crete and possessed a navy that was considered the most formidable in the ancient Mediterranean. His navy gave him the power to exert a considerable amount of influence over the Aegean Sea, establish colonies on the Aegean Islands, and suppress piracy, which ensured safe passage for Minoan traders and seafarers.

The most notable mythological accounts come from Thucydides and Plutarch and tell tales of Minos's navy and how it was the tool with which he established Crete's dominance in the region. It was one of the earliest thalassocracies (sea empires) in recorded history. This thalassocracy was the key to Minos's military and economic control.

The actual historical existence of King Minos and the exact degree of his naval power is heavily debated among historians and archaeologists. The Minoan civilization is well documented and had a known naval prowess and extensive trade networks. However, direct evidence of an incredibly powerful navy or Minos's rule is elusive. Most of it is rooted in mythology and legendary accounts. There aren't many concrete archaeological findings. What we do know from surviving frescoes is that the Minoan navy didn't consist of a bunch of warships. They looked more like the standard merchant fleet of the period but had marines or warriors on board too.

Crete was an ideal location for ancient maritime trade. The influence of Minoan civilization can be found everywhere in the Mediterranean, with their art and artistic styles popping up in ports from Greece to Egypt. Their art depicted animals, sea battles, and rituals that surrounded the sea.

By examining paintings and archeological evidence, we know that Minoan ships were around thirty-five meters long and six meters at their widest point. Each side could hold twenty-five oars for propulsion. Each ship would be fully provisioned with 120 men, the shipmaster, and his team of specialists. Each ship had a cargo capacity of around fifty metric tons.

The Minoans used large cypress trees that were cut and shaped by bronze tools and steam. Each board would be fitted together with tenon joints that were cut to fit snugly, and the joint was further solidified with a mixture of resins. The Minoans used wooden pegs to further strengthen the joints. Their methods required very little caulking. Once the ship was completed, the sea would cause the cypress wood to swell and create watertight seams. Once the wood construction was complete, they covered the outside of the hull in a tightly woven and treated linen that had been painted white and decorated with artistic scenes of the sea, like dolphins and sea birds.

The Phoenicians

The Phoenician civilization became a seafaring people between 1500 and 332 BCE. The Phoenicians occupied what we now know as Lebanon and the coastlines of Syria and Israel. They excelled at constructing advanced vessels and maritime navigation, creating expansive trade networks not only across the Mediterranean but also into the Atlantic Ocean.

The durable and technologically advanced Phoenician ships came in two primary types: cargo ships called gauloi and warships. Their cargo ships had rounded hulls and a large central sail. Their warships were sleeker and designed more for speed and maneuverability. They came in two designs: galleys and lighter vessels. The galleys themselves were constructed in two designs. Biremes were set up with two rows of oars on each side, allowing for greater speed. Triremes were a later model that allowed for three rows of oars on each side. Many of the warships had a bronze battering ram affixed to the prow.

The Phoenicians not only became a dominant force in trade, but they were also fully equipped to engage in naval warfare. Their ships, expert navigation using astronomical observations, and intimate knowledge of the Mediterranean's current and wind patterns gave them everything they needed to establish colonies and trading posts along the coasts of North Africa, southern Europe, and beyond the Strait of Gibraltar.

Famous voyages, such as the circumnavigation of Africa ordered by Egyptian Pharaoh Necho II around 600 BCE and expeditions to Britain, underscore the Phoenicians' bold maritime ventures. These expeditions were driven by the desire to expand trade routes and discover new resources, illustrating their strategic use of naval power to enhance their economic and cultural influence throughout the ancient world.

The decline of Phoenician naval power began with the rise of competing powers, such as the Greeks and later the Romans, culminating in Alexander the Great's conquest of Tyre in 332 BCE, which marked a significant blow to Phoenician independence and maritime dominance.

Chapter 2 – Triremes and Tyrants

In the 5th and 4th centuries BCE, Athens was at the peak of its cultural and naval power. This was the golden age of Athens. Significant developments were being made across all aspects of societal life, from drama and sculpture to architecture and philosophy. This was the period of Athens that you read about in school history books. Statesmen like Pericles transformed the city and advanced democracy, but they also championed an ambitious program of public works. The most famous of these was the construction of the Parthenon on the Acropolis.

Athens had to be able to afford these cultural endeavors, so it needed an expansive foreign policy, which was made possible by its powerful navy. The Athenian navy was a military force first and foremost, but it also stood as an emblem of their identity and imperial ambitions. Athens became capable of controlling the Aegean Sea and exerted its influence over a vast empire that extended throughout the Mediterranean. Their power was rooted in the city's innovative strategies when it came to maritime travel and their adoption of the trireme, a fast and agile warship that became the fleet's backbone.

Athens Naval Expansion

Athens achieved this incredible naval power thanks to the father of naval warfare, Themistocles. Themistocles was born into a society that was teetering between aristocratic traditions and democratic ideals. He emerged as a champion of the common people and used his popular influence to mold Athens into a maritime powerhouse.

Around 483 BCE, there was a significant discovery of silver in the Laurion mines. Themistocles wanted to invest this economic discovery into building a formidable fleet of two hundred triremes. He faced some considerable opposition. First was the cost, but he countered that argument with the silver mines. Secondly, the strength of Athens lay in its land-based defenses, which had long been the backbone of its military strength. Political rivalries also posed a problem because his opponents didn't want the lower classes to have more power. A strong navy required a large number of rowers, and these rowers came from the lower classes. The fear was that a navy would increase the political power of the poorer citizens. Lastly, many Athenians did not understand the threat of Persia and thought Themistocles was overreacting.

Themistocles was focused on external threats, the most notable being the Persian Empire. Persian domination, or the potential of it, struck a lot of fear in the people of Athens and was a catalyzing force that pushed Athens toward strengthening its naval forces. Themistocles pushed to improve their navy and to construct a new and more strategic port facility at Piraeus. Piraeus then became a secured military harbor and also a thriving commercial hub, a perfect example of Athens' economic prosperity.

The transformation under Themistocles was profound—militarily, economically, and politically—setting the stage for what would be considered the golden age of Athens. His leadership navigated Athens through immediate existential threats and laid the foundational structures that would propel the city-state into a period of unprecedented cultural and political flourishing.

The Role of Triremes in Asserting Athenian Dominance

Triremes were instrumental in establishing Athenian naval supremacy in the ancient Mediterranean. This ship, which is easily recognized by its three banks of oars, was an incredibly successful tool in key battles, cementing Athens as a dominant maritime power.

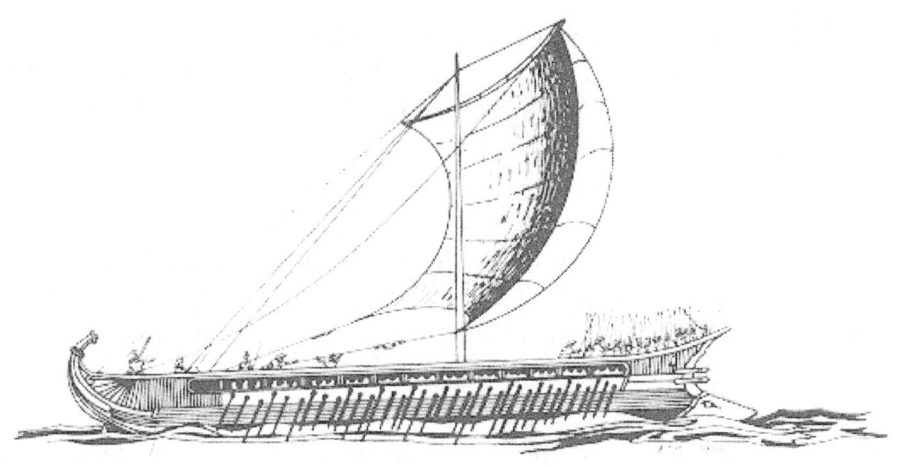

An illustration of a Greek trireme. [ii]

The triremes' design gave these ships exceptional maneuverability and speed. Each trireme typically carried a crew that included rowers who were arranged into three tiers. The thranites were at the top, zygites in the middle, and thalamites at the bottom. Arranging the rowers this way allowed for more effective propulsion and quick maneuvering. These rowers were then complemented by a group of soldiers, which included hoplites and archers for boarding actions. Any steering was managed by two large oars, which made the trireme a highly responsive vessel for its size.

Athens led the Delian League, an alliance put together to counter the threat of the Persians. This alliance later evolved into the Athenian Empire. The triremes patrolled the Aegean Sea and projected the power of Athens for everyone to see. They controlled the trade routes and collected tributes from other Greek city-states. These ships were able to exert influence well outside their own shores.

The Greco-Persian Wars

The Greco-Persian Wars were a series of conflicts fought between the Greek city-states and the growing Persian Empire during the 5th century BCE.

Battle of Artemisium (480 BCE)

Xerxes I had amassed a massive Persian army and navy with the sole intent of conquering Greece and its city-states. Alongside the famous Battle of Thermopylae, there was the lesser-known Battle of Artemisium. Artemisium lay along the narrow straits of Euboea and provided a tactically strategic location against the larger Persian fleet. The Greek fleet was definitely outnumbered, but this location provided the perfect point to block the Persian naval forces off and protect the northern flank of the army at Thermopylae.

The Persian fleet had been battered by a storm, which is reported to have destroyed a third of their ships. At Artemisium, the Greek navy, led by commanders like Themistocles and the Spartan Eurybiades, was prepared to engage. However, even with the storms, the Greeks were outnumbered. The Greek fleet was well coordinated, and they used their superior tactics to counter the Persian efforts.

The battle lasted several days, and both fleets clashed in unfavorable conditions that tested everyone's capabilities and strategic ingenuity. The Greeks were experts at maneuverability, and they could use their knowledge of the local conditions to their utmost advantage. The Persians made a noble attempt to encircle and overwhelm the Greek ships, but this tactic proved ineffective in confined waters.

After three days, history can't say that either side decisively won this battle. It was a tactical stalemate but considered a strategic victory for Persia. It can be said that the battle was also strategically beneficial for the Greeks. They were able to stall the Persian navy and prevent them from joining forces with their land troops at Thermopylae. They also learned what tactics worked against the Persian navy, which they later used in their more successful campaigns, like the Battle of Salamis.

The Greeks eventually decided to withdraw from Artemisium, a move that was believed to be made after they received the news of the fall of Thermopylae.

The Battle of Salamis

One of the most celebrated naval engagements was the Battle of Salamis in 480 BCE. The outcome of this battle not only shaped Greek independence but also the downfall of the Persian Empire's ambitions in Europe.

Themistocles's master strategy required the navy to draw the larger Persian fleet into the confined waters of the Saronic Gulf near Salamis. Here, the Persians' numbers and size would put them at a disadvantage. The Athenians arranged their fleet so that their strategic strength was fully maximized. The triremes had superior maneuverability and were much better suited to close-quarter combat tactics.

King Xerxes I was easily lured into the strait under the pretense that the Greek forces were completely disorganized and retreating. Themistocles masterminded this deception perfectly by feeding misinformation to Xerxes through a Greek messenger, Sicinnus.

Once the Persians fell for this deceitful trick, the battle was underway. The Persians were instantly made vulnerable to the agile Greek triremes. The Greek ships employed tactics like *diekplous* (breaking through the enemy lines) and *periplous* (outflanking maneuvers), isolating and attacking the Persian vessels. The Greeks caused substantial damage to the Persian fleet.

The victory at Salamis demonstrated the effectiveness of strategic geographic positioning and innovative tactics when it came to naval warfare. It also set the stage for further Greek successes against the Persians at Plataea and Mycale. The Greeks effectively ended the Persian invasion of Greece, beginning the ascendancy of Athens as a major power in the Mediterranean.

Battle of Mycale (479 BCE)

The Battle of Mycale was a decisive battle during the second Persian invasion of Greece. Again, this naval battle is often overshadowed by the larger land battle, this time the Battle of Platea, which saw the Greek forces, consisting mainly of Spartans, Athenians, and Corinthians, defeat the Persians.

This Greek fleet was under the command of Spartan King Leotychides and the Athenian commander Xanthippus. The Ionians suggested an assault on the Persian navy stationed at Mycale on the coast of Ionia. They believed an attack at this moment in time and in this area would inspire the Greek city-states that had fallen under Persian control to rebel against their colonizers.

When the Greeks arrived, they found the Persian fleet beached. The Persians had secured their vessels behind a palisade that was guarded by a substantial Persian army. The Greeks chose to attack anyway, executing a direct assault on the Persian positions. The Greek troops, with their heavily armored hoplites, were superior in combat and overwhelmed the Persian forces. Many Ionian Greek contingents that were within the Persian ranks defected to the Greek side, just as the Ionians had hoped for.

This was a two-fold win for the Greeks. The hoplites attached to the Greek navy crushed the Persian army stationed there and captured and destroyed the Persian fleet. With the accompanying win at Plataea, they effectively ended any Persian ambitions in Greece. With two successful campaigns against the Persians, the Greeks went on the offensive instead of the defensive. They started a new phase in the Greco-Persian Wars, where they targeted Persian territories in the Aegean Sea and Ionia.

Battle of the Eurymedon (469 or 466 BCE)

This battle, which was fought in either 469 or 466 BCE, was a joint effort between the naval Delian League, led by the Athenian general Cimon, and the Persian Empire near the Eurymedon River in Pamphylia, Asia Minor.

After the Greco-Persian Wars, tensions with Persia continued. The Delian League, an alliance between the city-states of Greece, had been created by Athens to liberate Greek cities from Persian control and secure trade routes.

Cimon decided to run an outrageous campaign against the Persian forces, which started by targeting the city-states in Asia Minor. Cimon was in charge of a formidable fleet of two hundred ships and managed to challenge Persian dominance in the area far more easily than anyone had anticipated.

The Battle of the Eurymedon started as a naval encounter and ended with a surprise land attack. Cimon was aggressive. At the mouth of the Eurymedon River, he defeated the Persian navy through aggressive maneuvers. The Persians attempted to avoid any confrontation until reinforcements arrived, but Cimon pushed them, forcing them into combat. As before, the Persians held the numbers but were not as capable as the Greeks in these confined spaces and suffered heavy losses.

Cimon didn't want to give the Persians any time to recover. Once he won on water, he landed his forces, launching a night attack on the Persian camp. The Persians were taken by surprise. The Greek forces quickly overwhelmed the Persians, who were killed or fled.

Not only did this decisive victory weaken Persia's naval power, but it also emboldened the confidence and prestige of the Delian League. It's the perfect demonstration of the power of combined naval and land tactics.

Battle of Aegospotami (405 BCE)

This decisive naval engagement occurred during the Peloponnesian War between Athens and Sparta. It ended as a catastrophic loss for the

Athenians and ultimately led to the fall of the Athenian Empire.

The Athenian navy, led by Admiral Conon, was stationed near the mouth of the Hellespont (now the Dardanelles). The opposing Spartan fleet, led by Lysander, was based across the strait at Lampsacus. The Athenians depended on their naval superiority in the area to secure the grain shipments that they needed for the city to survive. Lysander fully understood this vulnerability and sought to break this lifeline for the Athenians.

Lysander was incredibly strategic and had the full backing of the Persian financial empire, which allowed him to rebuild and maintain a formidable fleet for Sparta. The Athenian fleet tried over several days to draw Lysander's forces into battle, but Lysander didn't fall for their tricks. Every three days, the Athenians would sail out in formation to confront Lysander. Lysander refused to engage, which caused the Athenians to retreat back to their base without achieving any confrontation.

By the fifth day, Lysander took the offensive, launching a devastating surprise attack. As the Athenian fleet followed its usual routine, the Athenians left their ships largely unmanned while they foraged for food on shore. Lysander seized this opportunity. While they were ashore, he attacked their unguarded ships, capturing or destroying almost the entire fleet. This was a sudden and brutal strike that left Athens without any means to sustain its food supplies, much less communicate with its territories. It crippled the city-state.

Athens' situation was dire. This devastating blow led to the siege and subsequent surrender of Athens in 404 BCE. It marked the shift in power in the area to Sparta, which significantly altered the balance of power in ancient Greece. This defeat marked the end of Athenian naval dominance and the dramatic fall of its democratic empire. The region shifted closer to a Spartan hegemony, even though this would not last long. Continued conflicts and shifting alliances in Greece persisted.

Naval Power and Greek Culture

The success of Athenian democracy can be directly linked to the development and maintenance of naval power. Significant naval victories, like those during the Persian wars, elevated Athens into a position of leadership among the Greek city-states. The Persian threat led to the establishment of the Delian League. The league was originally developed to deter further Persian invasions but ultimately served to extend the Athenian hegemony across the Aegean Sea. On the same note, the reliance on naval supremacy also created a form of imperialism that was often at odds with the democratic ideal that Athens put forth. This contradiction played a role in the eventual decline of Athenian democracy. The empire's aggressive expansion ended up alienating allies and created conflicts like the Peloponnesian War.

Greek city-states like Athens were heavily dependent on their naval capabilities for their economic prosperity. Maritime trade not only facilitated the exchange of goods but also ideas and cultural practices across the Mediterranean and the Black Sea. Greek ships transported olive oil, wine, and pottery to distant ports while importing grains and metals that they needed to sustain their population and armies. The Athenians' control of the sea routes was what allowed them to flourish economically. The city's monumental architecture and sponsorship of the arts and philosophy were made possible by its navy and warships. The wealth generated from their maritime trade funded the city's defensive capabilities and public projects, which employed large portions of the population, which then reinforced the democratic process.

The strategic and economic importance of naval power had a profound and lasting impact on the development of Greek society. It affected everything from military strategy and political configurations to economic policies and culture. Their naval prowess was a linchpin in Greece's cultural and political developments, shaping the histories and destinies of every city-state.

Chapter 3 – The Roman Naval Dominance

Initially, the Romans were not a maritime power. Their early naval activities were limited and largely focused on small-scale operations meant to secure coastal areas and suppress piracy. As the Romans' commercial interests and territorial ambitions expanded, there came a need for a more durable and strong naval presence. This was especially so in response to the threat posed by Carthage during the Punic Wars.

Rome's initial steps toward securing access to the sea started with the establishment of colonies as strategic coastal locations, like Ostia and Antium, in the 4th century BCE. This was the first time Rome obviously acknowledged the importance of naval power. These sites could not have been effectively defended without a capable fleet, which hints at the idea that early naval engagements were likely driven by necessity rather than a strategic maritime vision.

Naval Engineering and Ship Design

Roman naval capabilities transformed during the First Punic War. The Romans shifted from focusing on land-based military supremacy to establishing a formidable presence at sea. Rome's initial fleet was rudimentary. It was tailored more for coastal patrol than any major sea battles. When they were confronted with Carthage's superior naval forces, which had dominated Mediterranean trade and warfare up to this point, Rome was compelled to enhance its own military maritime capabilities.

Carthage's naval prowess was significantly anchored on the quinquereme. These were large warships that were known for their durability and the substantial number of marines they could carry. The Romans managed to capture a Carthaginian quinquereme, and their engineers extensively studied it to reverse engineer the process of building one so they could replicate the design.

The quinquereme featured multiple rows of oars in a large hull that was capable of bearing the weight of a great number of soldiers along with the necessary provisions for extended naval engagements. The adoption of this ship by Rome allowed the Romans to rapidly build a fleet of 120 ships, a move that significantly bolstered its naval strength.

After copying Carthaginian strength at sea, Rome began to make significant innovations of its own. The corvus was a revolutionary boarding device and potentially the most significant contribution Rome made to naval warfare. The corvus functioned as a bridge that could be lowered onto enemy ships during battle. One end of the corvus was spiked so that it would hook onto the opponent's deck, allowing Roman soldiers to board and engage in close combat. This ingenious move allowed Roman soldiers to utilize the superior infantry tactics they had developed on land. They first demonstrated this innovation and how well it worked at the Battle of Mylae in 260 BCE.

How the corvus worked. [iii]

The corvus saw some incredible early success. However, it had a major drawback. By locking with the Carthaginian ships, it compromised the stability of the Roman ships. It made them more susceptible to capsizing and rough seas. So, the use of the corvus was a double-edged sword. While it offered immense tactical advantages in combat, it risked maritime safety. Roman naval strategists recognized this problem and eventually phased out the corvus. They sought other means to leverage their infantry's capabilities that wouldn't jeopardize their fleets.

After the Punic Wars, Roman shipbuilding continued to evolve with advancements in hull designs, rigging, and the use of multiple masts to improve their navigability and speed. Their navy was now more capable of longer voyages and more complex military operations. This continuous improvement underscored the Roman commitment to maintaining maritime superiority. They adapted their designs and tactics from previous naval campaigns.

The Roman approach to naval warfare, characterized by rapid adaptation, technical innovation, and strategic ingenuity, was integral to their dominance in the Mediterranean. It allowed them to protect their burgeoning empire and to protect their power far beyond the Italian Peninsula. Ultimately, they were able to control major maritime trade routes and influence the political landscape of the region.

Expansion and Dominance of the Roman Navy

As Rome's ambitions grew, its navy evolved from mere auxiliary units into legions and then into a dominant maritime force. Control over Sicily was crucial for their military prestige and for economic reasons. It opened avenues for trade and agriculture. The Roman strategy for dominance involved securing vital trade routes and establishing control over strategic islands like Sicily, Sardinia, and Corsica. The strategy effectively pushed Carthage out of its strongholds in the western Mediterranean, shifting the balance of power considerably to Rome.

The First Punic War

The First Punic War, fought from 264 to 241 BCE, was the pivotal moment in Roman history when the Romans turned into a formidable naval power. This conflict was primarily fought over control of Sicily and saw some of the largest naval engagements in ancient history. It also led to major innovations in Roman naval tactics and shipbuilding.

Battle of Mylae (260 BCE)

As mentioned previously, the Battle of Mylae was Rome's first major naval victory using the corvus. This naval battle took place off the coast of northern Sicily near Mylae (modern Milazzo). Gaius Duilius commanded the Roman forces against the Carthaginian fleet led by Hannibal Gisco.

Before this encounter, Rome had limited experience in naval warfare, especially when compared to the seasoned Carthaginian navy. Carthage held dominance at sea. The Carthaginians were able to conduct raids all along the Italian coast and Sicily. In response, Rome built a large fleet, modeling it after their own.

The corvus won Rome this battle. Roman soldiers were capable now of boarding and capturing Carthaginian ships. They were able to neutralize the Carthaginians' naval experience and turn a naval battle into a land battle.

During the encounter, the Romans were able to capture the Carthaginian flagship and several other vessels, which significantly hampered the Carthaginian fleet's effectiveness. The Carthaginians fought valiantly but were unable to counter this new boarding technique created by the Romans. The Romans were able to capture thirty-one Carthaginian ships and sink thirteen others. This battle boosted Roman morale and marked a shift in control of the Sicilian waters from Carthage to Rome.

After a victory like this, it's no wonder that the Romans had confidence in their naval capabilities. The battle was such a success that Gaius Duilius was honored with a triumph in Rome, and a rostral column was erected in the Forum to commemorate the victory.

Battle of Cape Ecnomus (256 BCE)

This battle occurred off the southern coast of Sicily in 256 BCE. It ranks up there as one of the largest naval battles in ancient history. This confrontation occurred between the Roman Republic, under the command of consuls Marcus Atilius Regulus and Lucius Manulis Vulso Longus, and the Carthaginian fleet, which was commanded by Hanno the Great and Hamilcar Barca.

Rome decided it needed to challenge Carthage's dominance at sea even more to successfully invade North Africa. Once they made the decision, they began constructing a massive fleet of 330 warships. The Carthaginians countered this powerful navy by assembling 350 ships of their own to intercept the Romans and prevent them from landing in Africa.

The Roman tactical formation for this battle was highly innovative. They arranged their massive fleet in a triangular formation that was designed to penetrate the Carthaginian lines forcefully, much like an army on land. The Romans divided their ships into four squadrons. The lead ships formed the apex of the triangle and were to engage the enemy directly. They were backed by a reserve force to reinforce them when needed. This formation allowed the Romans to maintain a unified front. The strategy was sound and made it very difficult for the Carthaginians to exploit any weaknesses.

The Carthaginians planned to use their superior maneuverability and experienced crews to outflank and encircle the Roman formation. This caused them to stretch their lines thin.

The battle resulted in a decisive victory for Rome. The Carthaginians suffered significant losses, losing over one hundred ships, while Rome only lost twenty-four. The Roman naval forces celebrated this victory by sending the prows of the captured ships to Rome to adorn the speaker's platform (the Rostra) in the Forum.

With this success, Rome was able to land an army in Africa and put Carthage on the defensive, helping to shift the balance of naval power in the Mediterranean.

Battle of Drepana (249 BCE)

While these other battles were successes, the Battle of Drepana was a defeat for Rome. Carthage's navy, under the command of Adherbal, was formidable. At this time, the Roman fleet was led by Publius Claudius Pulcher, who decided to attempt a surprise attack on a Carthaginian fleet moored at Drepana (modern Trapani). This decision backfired disastrously.

Claudius was trying to capitalize on a strategic advantage by launching this surprise attack. He tried to trap the Carthaginian ships in the harbor at Drepana. However, he timed this poorly. This poor timing, combined with adverse omens that affected the Romans, set the stage for catastrophe. An example of a bad omen was an incident where Claudius threw sacred chickens overboard after they refused to eat.

As the Roman fleet approached their destination, their ships became scattered in the dark. They lost the element of surprise as a result. Adherbal seized the opportunity and quickly maneuvered his fleet out of the harbor into a much more favorable position to counterattack. The Romans were already struggling and were hindered by the dark and found themselves pinned against the shore. They found themselves in the exact position they had hoped to put the Carthaginians in.

The Carthaginian ships were better crewed and far more maneuverable. A significant number of Roman ships were either captured or destroyed, once again demonstrating Carthage's naval superiority.

The defeat at Drepana was a major setback for Rome. The Romans' overconfidence and lack of preparation only proved how superior the Carthaginians were in regard to naval tactics. At this point, Rome temporarily withdrew from large-scale naval engagements against Carthage. It took several years before Rome could rebuild its fleet and challenge Carthage's dominance at sea once again.

The Battle of the Aegates (241 BCE)

On March 10th, 241 BCE, the Roman fleet, commanded by Gaius Lutatius Catullus, attacked the Carthaginian fleet led by Hanno near the Aegates Islands (off the western coast of Sicily). The Carthaginians were trying to relieve their besieged strongholds in Sicily and were caught off-guard by the Romans. The Romans had stripped all of their ships of unnecessary weight to make them faster at sea, so they were able to outmaneuver the heavier and supply-laden Carthaginian ships. Catullus also deliberately chose the location and waited for favorable weather to strike.

This battle was devastating for Carthage. About half of their fleet was completely destroyed or captured by the Romans. Carthage was forced to seek peace, leading to the Treaty of Lutatius, which stipulated heavy reparations and demanded the Carthaginians evacuate Sicily. This battle successfully made Sicily a Roman province.

From Carthage to Piracy

Rome's naval battle against piracy began sporadically. Part of this was due to the fact that the Roman elites often benefited from the pirates' activities. One notable commander was Marcus Antonius Creticus, the father of the triumvirate Mark Anthony. He undertook a campaign against piracy, which resulted in little to no significant change.

The threat of piracy remained largely unchecked throughout the Roman Republic. Their approach to piracy was more reactive rather than proactive, and they struggled to implement a consistent strategy, which made piracy a plague on their trade and military routes.

The issue with piracy reached a tipping point in the later Roman Republic when it started impacting the grain supply that was crucial to Rome's subsistence. The Roman Senate granted Pompey the Great considerable power in 67 BCE under the Lex Gabinia. This allowed Pompey to organize a significant military initiative against the pirate menace, hopefully one that would be far more successful than his contemporary Creticus.

Pompey started by dividing the Mediterranean into sectors. Each sector would be patrolled by parts of a substantial fleet that consisted of 500 ships and around 120,000 men. A coordinated and focused effort was made to cleanse each area of pirates before moving on to the next one. This effectively isolated and eliminated pirate activity sector by sector. The claim was made that Pompey's approach cleared the western Mediterranean of pirates in just forty days. The success continued as he attacked the pirate strongholds in Cilicia, captured their bases, and decisively defeated them.

Pompey offered the defeated pirates opportunities for resettlement so they could become farmers. However, the caveat was that their farms would be located in regions far from the coast. The pirates were subsequently removed from their maritime bases of operations and reintegrated into Roman society. The idea was to make it impossible for them to return to their former way of life.

Pompey's campaign against piracy was a critical turning point that restored Roman control over the Mediterranean. This naval dominance over pirates ensured the safety of maritime trade routes and secured the economic interests of the Roman Republic.

Establishing an Imperial Navy

The establishment of the imperial Roman navy by Augustus marked a significant evolution in Roman military strategy. It transformed the Roman military into a permanent force that was dedicated primarily to controlling the Mediterranean, ensuring safe trade routes, and supporting military logistics across the empire's vast territories.

The Battle of Actium (31 BCE)

This all began after Augustus's victory at the Battle of Actium in 31 BCE. This battle was a monumental naval confrontation that marked the end of the Roman Republic and the beginning of Rome's imperial era under Augustus. The battle took place near Actium in Greece. The forces of Octavian (who would later be known as Augustus) went against the allied forces of Mark Antony and Cleopatra VII of Egypt.

Mark Anthony and Cleopatra assembled a large fleet and a substantial army. However, their strategic position was compromised by several factors, including defections to Octavian's side and logistical challenges. Anthony's fleet was superior in number, but he did not have enough men to man them all. His fleet also consisted of large warships that were less maneuverable than Octavian's lighter and more agile vessels. Octavian's general, Marcus Agrippa, played a vital role in the conflict, as he used the smaller, more maneuverable Liburnian ships to cut off Anthony's supplies and isolate his forces.

A liburna was a style of ship originating with the Liburnians, an ancient Illyrian tribe known for their shipbuilding skills. These were light, fast, and highly maneuverable galley warships. The Romans adopted and adapted the design for their military under Agrippa. Liburnae were smaller and lighter than the traditional triremes and quinqueremes. They were quick-strike ships that typically had a single bank of oars. In some cases, the Romans adapted the model to give them more power with more rowers. The deck was also reinforced for fighting so that their marines could aid in boarding actions.

The battle began when Anthony attempted to break the naval blockade imposed by Octavian. The battle was fierce, and Cleopatra and Anthony eventually fled to Egypt. Octavian was then able to consolidate power and establish control over Rome and its territories. He soon declared himself Augustus, marking the dawn of the Roman Empire.

Octavian used the victory at Actium as a propaganda tool. He promoted his role as the savior of Rome from Eastern influences and the decadence represented by Anthony and Cleopatra. The victory established his political power and led to the annexation of Egypt. After Egypt became a Roman province, it provided a vital grain supply for Rome. This event also paved the way for the Pax Romana, a long period of relative peace and stability across the Roman Empire.

Imperial Navy

Following the victory at Actium, Augustus recognized the need for a strong naval presence to maintain his control over the Mediterranean. At this point, the Mediterranean had become a "Roman lake." After his victory, he restructured the naval force into a more organized and permanent entity. This newly established imperial navy was centered around two major fleet bases: Classis Misenensis at Misenum in the Bay of Naples and Classis Ravennas at Ravenna on the Adriatic coast. The locations of these bases were chosen since they were perfectly located to control the main maritime routes and protect vital grain supplies from North Africa.

The imperial navy did more than just patrol and secure maritime routes; it also served as logistical support for the Roman legions. The navy transported troops and supplies, which was crucial for maintaining the stability and reach of the empire. This was most especially true during military campaigns in regions like Spain and North Africa and, later, in Britain and along the Rhine and Danube Rivers. The fleet ensured that Rome could protect its power, maintain its interests across the Mediterranean, and stretch to the vast edges of the empire.

Under Augustus, the navy saw an expansion in roles and responsibilities. This included safeguarding new provinces and suppressing piracy, which continued to be a problem despite Pompey's earlier successes. Being proactive helped secure Roman economic interests and stabilized regions that were critical to Rome's grain supply, most notably Egypt. Augustus reportedly founded the Alexandrine fleet, which was specifically designed to safeguard Egypt.

The Decline of Roman Naval Power

During the height of its power, Rome's navy was essential in securing the Mediterranean and supporting its military campaigns. However, after the naval battles of the First and Second Punic Wars, the strategic focus on naval power began to wane. This isn't to say that they no longer had a military focus at all; rather, their focus shifted from naval warfare to securing trade and maritime dominance. As they conquered significant maritime threats, a gradual decline in naval engagement and innovation began. Without significant maritime threats, Rome did not see a reason to focus on naval prowess anymore. The Roman navy transitioned toward a more policing role, patrolling trade routes and combating piracy rather than engaging in large-scale naval battles, though they did happen.

This shift was only exacerbated by internal conflicts, especially during the periods of civil war within the Roman Republic. Naval activities were often sidelined in favor of more pressing military engagements on land. The Romans began to rely more on provincial fleets and allied forces for maritime patrols, which diminished the role of the Roman state in maintaining naval affairs. Even with the establishment of the imperial navy, the Romans never regained the prominence it once had. The fleet's role was mostly confined to coast guard functions and logistical support.

Chapter 4 – The Viking Longships

Viking longships were renowned for their sleek and formidable design and were critical to the Norse seafarers' dominance over the northern European waters from the late 8th to the early 11th centuries CE. These ships allowed the Vikings to engage in exploration, trade, and warfare over vast distances.

Longship Speed and Capabilities

Viking longships were swift. They could reach up to seventeen knots in favorable conditions, a significant advantage for both raiding and trading expeditions. By using both sails and oars, these ships could maneuver effectively in all different maritime scenarios. When using the sails, they could harness the wind to achieve high speeds across open waters, and the oars allowed for controlled navigation in calmer or more congested waters like rivers or during battles.

Viking longships were constructed using the clinker method. Overlapping wooden planks were riveted together to form a strong and flexible hull. The Vikings used lightweight materials like oak to create the vessels. Their ships were sleek and streamlined. Their length-to-breath ratio was typically around 7:1, significantly improving their speed and maneuverability.

What really set the Vikings apart was their navigation innovations. The Vikings were able to take long-distance voyages all the way to North America. Viking navigators used a blend of celestial navigation, landmark recognition, and environmental cues like wave patterns and marine life behavior to help guide their way. Some evidence suggests they had rudimentary navigational aids like the sun compass and sunstones to locate the sun's position during overcast conditions. This extensive amount of knowledge allowed them to travel confidently away from their coastlines and explore new territories across the ocean.

The structural design of the longships allowed them to operate in all different bodies of water. Viking ships could easily travel between the sea and a river, unlike other naval vessels. Their shallow draft allowed them to shift from open seas to rivers and even perform beach landings quickly and easily. All of this was incredibly important to their raiding activities. This ship design allowed the Vikings to surprise their enemies by approaching from waterways that were not typically navigable by larger vessels of that era.

Construction

Viking longships are the perfect example of masterful engineering. Wooden planks, known as strakes, were fastened together using iron or wood rivets. These planks were often made from oak, which was chosen for its durability and resistance to the harsh maritime conditions of the North Sea. The natural curve of oak trees was exploited to match the desired curvature of the ship's hull.

After these planks were installed, the Vikings had to ensure the ships were watertight. They stuffed the gaps between the planks with tarred wool and animal hair. This technique prevented water from entering the ship and contributed to the ship's overall structural integrity. Another key aspect was the use of radially split wood. The planks that built these ships followed the natural grain of wood, which enhanced strength and durability.

The sail was typically made from wool and was square shaped. The Vikings attached it to a tall central mast. They used a single large sail to catch the wind, which propelled the ship. They also rowed using oars. By today's standards, their rigging system was rudimentary, as it consisted of ropes made from natural fibers that controlled the sail's position relative to the wind. Viking rigging used basic ropes that adjusted the position of a single sail. The sail could be adjusted to a more beneficial angle relative to the winds, and these movements were limited. Depending on the wind, this could reduce the ship's ability to move effectively. Modern sailboats have far more complex rigging systems that can raise and lower the sail, control the tension of the sail, and stabilize the mast when fully capturing the wind. A Viking sail could only be roughly oriented; otherwise, they would have to reposition the entire sail, which was a laborious task.

Shipbuilding was a revered craft in Viking society. In many cases, it was an effort that involved the entire community. Shipbuilding techniques were passed down through the generations. Shipbuilders used timber for critical structural components like the keel, sterns, and ribs. This timber was carefully selected for the natural shapes that fit specific parts of the ship. This minimized weak points and maximized the strength of the vessel.

These longships were not purely functional. They also held significant symbolic and spiritual importance. Their prows were often ornately carved and typically shaped like dragons or serpents. These carvings were believed to protect sailors from sea monsters and evil spirits but were also used to intimidate enemies during raids. Their ships also played a crucial role in burial rituals. Many prominent Vikings were buried with their ships, which were seen as their vessel to the afterlife.

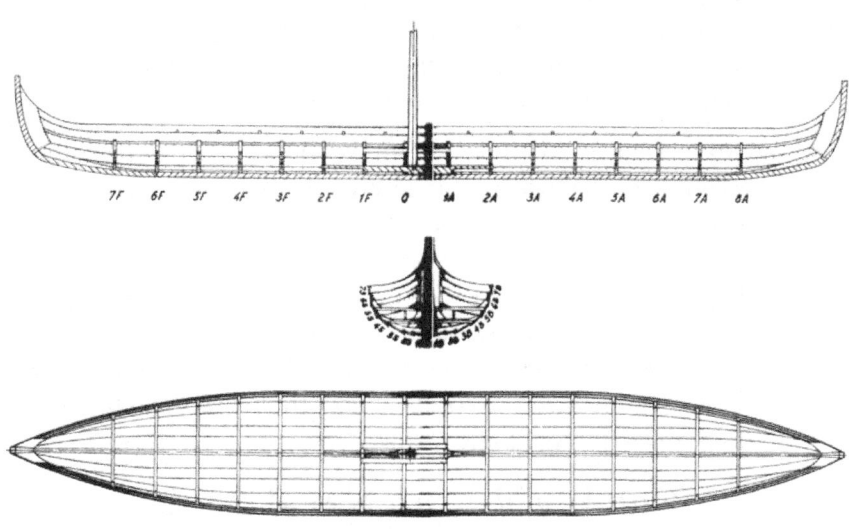

Schematic drawing of a Viking longship.[iv]

Viking Naval Activities: Raiding

The Vikings are often remembered for their fearsome raids and the terror that they spread across Europe, but their naval capabilities were equally remarkable and played a critical role in their military successes. Their naval warfare tactics and their shipbuilding techniques enabled them to launch attacks across vast distances. These capabilities led to profound geopolitical changes in medieval Europe.

Key Aspects of Viking Naval Warfare

- **Ship Design and Mobility:** The Viking longships had a shallow draft and an incredibly symmetrical design. These ships were fast, highly maneuverable, and capable of riverine and open sea navigation. This allowed the Vikings to execute surprise raids with remarkable efficiency. Their longships could land directly on beaches, which meant rapid deployment and retreat of their forces. Vikings usually engaged in hit-and-run, especially early on in the Viking Age.

- **Tactics and Strategy:** The Vikings readily used their speed, surprise, and knowledge of local waters to their advantage when it came to naval engagements. They would appear unexpectedly, attack swiftly, and then escape before local forces could muster an effective defense. This approach wasn't only effective in raids but also in larger naval battles where coordination and speed were critical.

- **Psychological Warfare:** The Vikings were very good at psychological warfare. The sight of Viking ships approaching was often enough to cause panic among coastal populations. The Vikings had established a reputation for brutality. Their distinctive ships were also often adorned with fearsome figureheads. Thus, a significant amount of psychological warfare often preceded actual combat. This fear was a tactical asset. It often led to easy victories since their opponents were too demoralized to fight effectively.

Notable Viking Naval Raids

The Viking Age was marked by numerous and audacious naval raids that left a lasting impact on Europe. These raids often started as a naval encounter and moved inland.

The Raid on Lindisfarne (793 CE)

One of the most well-known Viking raids occurred in 793 CE. Anyone who has looked into this particular period of history knows of the monastery of Lindisfarne, an island located off the northeast coast of England. The raid on Lindisfarne is often considered the beginning of the Viking Age. The attack on the monastery shocked the Christian West and marked the Vikings as a formidable threat due to their ability to strike swiftly and unpredictably from the sea.

The event was documented by Alcuin of York. Alcuin lamented how vulnerable the holy site was and described the horror of the attack, which signaled a new and terrifying chapter in European history.

Lindisfarne was a revered monastic community and center of learning. It was known for its rich religious life and as the home of Saint Cuthbert. The monastery was wealthy and filled with valuable liturgical artifacts and manuscripts, which made it an attractive target for the Norse raiders. As history tells us, the Viking attack was brutal. They came by sea, and they killed monks, looted treasures, and desecrated the church.

Alcuin interprets the attack as divine retribution for the sins of the people. His writings convey the profound sense of shock and violation felt by his contemporaries. This particular raid had significant psychological impact that went far beyond the immediate physical damage.

The raid at Lindisfarne heralded a new era of Viking expansionism that shaped the dynamics of European politics and warfare for centuries. The Viking raid underscored the vulnerability of coastal and riverine locations throughout Europe to seaborne attacks. New fortifications were constructed at vulnerable sites, and the people reevaluated how to defend themselves against such mobile and elusive foes.

The Siege of Paris (845 CE)

One of the most notable events in Viking history was the siege of Paris in 845 CE. The Vikings started interacting with the Frankish Empire in the early 800s. This particular siege was led by a Norse chieftain often identified as Ragnar Lodbrok, a man made famous by a popular TV series on the History Channel. Ragnar Lodbrok took a fleet of 120 Viking ships and sailed up the Seine. From here, he laid siege to Paris, a strategic move showcasing the Vikings' formidable naval capabilities.

When they reached Paris, they encountered little resistance. The city at the time was under the rule of King Charles the Bald and was ill-prepared for such an attack. The Norsemen's arrival coincided with Easter. It was a common Viking tactic to coincide attacks with Christian holidays. Attacking on Christian holidays or on Sundays during typical church times caught their defenders off-guard and allowed them to more easily plunder the city. This particular siege demonstrated how even well-fortified cities were vulnerable to the Viking forces.

While the Vikings were initially successful at Paris, this success was marred by a plague that struck their camp during the siege. According to some historical accounts, the Vikings took this illness as a sign of divine retribution. Still, the Vikings managed to extract a ransom of 7,000 livres or over 2,500 kilograms of silver and gold from Charles the Bald.

This was one of the first times the Vikings collected tribute, a strategy in which people paid the Viking raiders to avoid further plunder. European rulers employed this tactic repeatedly for almost two centuries. It was considered a pragmatic approach to the continuous Viking naval raids.

The siege impacted Frankish military strategy. Their response to this siege was to create new fortifications around Paris. Later, particularly during the famous siege of 885 to 886, these fortifications protected the city to the point where Paris withstood a Viking attack for over a year.

The Sacking of Seville (844 CE)

In the 840s, the Vikings extended their raids into the Iberian Peninsula. At this time, the Iberian Peninsula was under the control of the Umayyad Emirate of Córdoba.

The Vikings successfully sailed up the Guadalquivir River and captured Seville in early October after overcoming local defenses. The city was known for its wealth and strategic importance, but it suffered extensive ponding by the Norsemen.

The biggest problem with sneak attacks is that they can be successful, but if the force doesn't leave quickly enough, the locals have time to organize a counter-offensive. And that's exactly what happened in Seville. Emir Abd ar-Rahman II of Córdoba responded to the Viking attack by assembling a considerable force. This force ultimately defeated the Vikings in the Battle of Talyata in mid-November.

After his great success, Abd ar-Rahman II took proactive measures to prevent future attacks by enhancing Seville's fortifications and establishing a dedicated naval arsenal to improve defensive capabilities along the river, specifically against the Vikings. His measures proved very effective in thwarting any future Viking attempts to raid the region.

The Foundation of the Danelaw

The establishment of the Danelaw, a region of England under Danish law, was the result of a series of invasions and settlements by Danish Vikings. Starting in the 9th century, a series of Viking invasions into what is now England established a whole area under Danish control.

The foundation of the Danelaw is closely linked to the arrival of the Great Heathen Army in 865 CE. This wasn't a small reading party arriving by ship; it was a large force aiming for conquest. This army was led by notable leaders such as Ivar the Boneless and Halfdan Ragnarsson, who systematically took over large portions of England by using both land and naval tactics. The Vikings' ability to shift from sea to riverine environments meant that by 876, the Danes had established firm control over Northumbria and East Anglia and had even made significant inroads into Mercia.

The Legacy of the Viking Navy

The Viking Age spanned from the late 8th century to the early 11th century. It was marked by significant advancements in naval technology, particularly in shipbuilding. One of the most profound impacts of Viking ship design on medieval Europe was other cultures adopting these shipbuilding techniques. Viking ships were notably faster and more maneuverable than many of their contemporaries. The longship influenced the development of later medieval European ships, such as the cog and the carrack. While the cog played a crucial role in medieval trade, and the carrack became vital during the Age of Exploration, these ships were influenced by a mix of North Sea, Baltic, and Mediterranean shipbuilding traditions. Viking knarrs, designed for long-distance trade, shared similarities with later cargo ships, particularly their broad hulls for carrying heavy loads.

The Vikings established extensive trade networks that already reached across Europe into North Africa, Russia, and the Middle East. These routes facilitated the exchange of goods like furs, timber, silk, spices, and silver. The economic impact of these trade routes was significant. Not only did they contribute to the wealth of Viking societies and enable their expansion, but it also allowed them to establish settlements far from their Scandinavian homelands.

Chapter 5 – The Age of Exploration and Naval Expansion

The Age of Exploration, spanning from the 15th to the 17th centuries, was marked by significant advancements in ship design and navigation. These advancements in ship design and navigation technologies were intricately tied to the era's naval warfare strategies.

Tools That Changed the Sea

Caravel

The caravel was a pivotal change in shipbuilding. This new design featured a combination of square and lateen sails that enhanced maneuverability and speed. The caravel was particularly effective for long voyages across uncharted waters but was also adaptable to various wind conditions. These ships allowed for quick positioning and retreats during sea battles.

Carrack

The earliest versions of the carrack had three masts with square sails on the foremast and mainmast and a lateen, or triangular sail, on the mizzenmast (the mast just behind the mainmast). Later versions of these large ocean vessels were constructed with an additional fourth mast. Unlike earlier ships, the sides of the carrack were much higher. Combine these sides with the rounded hull, and you have a vessel perfect for sailing over the open seas.

Carracks and caravels were significantly larger than their predecessors, allowing them to carry large crews and a large number of goods and weapons. It was now possible to take long voyages across open oceans and establish trade networks with distant regions like the Americas, Africa, and Asia. The addition of advanced weaponry made them formidable warships.

Compass and Astrolabe

The compass and astrolabe are major additions to sea navigation. When exploring the vast and often featureless ocean, the compass provided a reliable means of determining direction. The astrolabe allowed sailors to measure the altitude of celestial bodies, which helped them determine latitude. Both of these tools reduced navigational errors and expanded the possibilities for oceanic exploration.

Galleons

The development of the galleon followed the caravel and the carrack and further revolutionized naval warfare. Galleons were large, multi-decked sailing ships that combined the cargo capacity of carracks with the speed and maneuverability of caravels. They were designed to carry substantial cargo and firepower with the advent of gunpowder. They were typically longer and sleeker ships compared to the carrack, with a distinctive elongated hull that made them more efficient on long voyages. This ship type became the backbone of European naval forces and was crucial in maintaining control over vast transoceanic trade routes and colonial territories.

Galleons were heavily armed ships with rows of cannons mounted on their lower decks. This allowed them to deliver devastating broadsides in naval battles. Unlike earlier ships, which relied on hand-to-hand combat or boarding maneuvers, galleons prioritized long-range firepower. Their forecastle and sterncastle (or aftercastle)—the raised platforms at the front and back—were smaller and lower than those on carracks. This reduced wind resistance and improved their stability. Galleons were far better suited for open-ocean warfare.

Galleons were enormous compared to many ships of their time. Some of them exceeded five hundred tons in displacement and carried dozens of cannons. For instance, Spain's famous *San Martín*, the flagship of the Spanish Armada, displaced between 1,000 and 1,100 tons and carried 48 heavy guns.

The shift to sailing ships equipped with heavy cannons necessitated new battle formations and strategies. The line-ahead (or line of battle) tactic, in which ships formed a single line to maximize their broadside fire, became a standard naval battle formation during this period. This formation emphasized the firepower of the galleons and was constantly used in naval conflicts, including the Anglo-Dutch Wars.

These changes in ship design and navigation enhanced maritime trade and transformed naval battles into grander, more strategic engagements. European powers could now project their power across the world and safeguard their trade routes and colonial interests against rivals. The naval arms race spurred by these technological innovations led to increased military conflicts on the seas.

Key Figures

The Age of Exploration saw some significant figures change naval exploration for future generations.

Christopher Columbus

Christopher Columbus made a historic and famous voyage in 1492. This voyage was sponsored by the Catholic monarchs of Spain, Isabella I of Castile and Ferdinand II of Aragon. Christopher Columbus set sail with the goal of finding a western route to Asia. However, as this voyage played out, Columbus instead landed in the Caribbean, ushering in a new era of European exploration and colonization of the Americas. This journey broadened the geographical horizons of Europe but had profound impacts on the Indigenous populations and ecological environments of the newly discovered lands.

Columbus's voyage led to widespread exploration and colonization efforts by several European powers. His journey was supported by significant financial investments from Spanish royals and European bankers. Maritime explorations were economic and strategic, and many wanted to be involved in this favorable venture.

Despite his navigational prowess, Columbus's life was marred by political and administrative challenges. He faced accusations of mismanagement in the colonies that he helped establish and was involved in legal battles over the privileges and titles granted to him by the Spanish Crown. So, even Columbus's naval accomplishments could not protect him from politics at home. His reputation diminished toward the end of his life and overshadowed the initial acclaim he received with his discovery of the Americas.

Vasco da Gama

Vasco da Gama's voyage took place five years after Columbus's first voyage. Da Gama was patronized by King Manuel I of Portugal. His journey found the first sea route from Europe to India by rounding Africa's Cape of Good Hope. This discovery revolutionized the spice trade and established Portugal as a major maritime power in the Indian Ocean.

Da Gama's voyage was motivated by the desire to find a direct sea route to the rich spice markets of Asia. The route overland was monotonous and took an incredible amount of time, and the Mediterranean routes were controlled by Islamic powers. Da Gama's successful navigation to Calicut on the southwest coast of India in 1498 opened up new avenues for European trade and colonization in Asia.

However, the interactions between the Portuguese and the local populations were not always peaceful. When Vasco da Gama first arrived in Calicut in 1498, he was initially welcomed by the Hindu ruler, the Zamorin, as the visit represented the first direct maritime contact with Europe. However, tensions emerged almost immediately due to misunderstandings and cultural differences. The gifts da Gama brought, including cheap trinkets and textiles, were seen as insulting by the Zamorin, who was accustomed to high-value trade goods like gold, spices, and silks. It was a misstep that strained relations, as it suggested that the Portuguese lacked respect for local customs and the wealth of the region.

The already-established Muslim traders in Calicut viewed the Portuguese as unwelcome competition. They dominated the lucrative spice trade and feared that the Portuguese would disrupt their networks by bypassing traditional overland routes that were controlled by Islamic powers. They actively resisted Portuguese efforts to establish a foothold, which only escalated the conflicts.

Da Gama's response was aggressive. His later voyages involved the use of European cannons to dominate and control trade routes. He often resorted to violence against local and Muslim trading vessels.

In 1502, da Gama returned armed with a fleet and royal backing. His approach changed to involve outright hostility to establish and secure a Portuguese monopoly over the spice trade. His fleet readily attacked Arab ships and imposed a reign of terror along the Malabar coast to subdue the local populations and rival traders. This included a notorious incident where da Gama captured a ship that was filled with Muslim pilgrims, including women and children, seizing its valuable cargo and setting the ship on fire. This resulted in the death of many of those on board.

In 1503, during what became known as the Battle of Calicut, da Gama engaged in a brutal conflict with the forces of Calicut. He used the superior firepower of European cannons to bombard the city. This attack resulted in heavy casualties and damage. This military aggression was a clear demonstration of naval power meant to intimidate and subdue the local rulers and ensure Portuguese dominance in the region.

These actions temporarily secured Portuguese objectives but also instilled long-lasting enmity and resistance among the local populations and the other trading powers that were affected by Portuguese incursions.

Da Gama's exploits laid the groundwork for Portugal's regional commercial monopoly. Strategic ports like Goa fortified Portugal's trading posts along the Indian coast, Malacca, and the Persian Gulf. The strategic use of naval power allowed Portugal to control the spice trade routes and assert its dominance over the Indian Ocean.

Ferdinand Magellan

Ferdinand Magellan set sail from Seville on August 10th, 1519. This monumental event in history would lead to the first successful circumnavigation of the globe. Unfortunately, Magellan did not survive the voyage, but his leadership and navigational skills were key throughout the journey.

The fleet first made its way to the Canary Islands and then passed the Cape Verde Islands, navigating along the West African coast. Magellan's aim was to find a passage through South America to reach the Pacific Ocean. This feat was realized with the discovery of what's now called the Strait of Magellan, which happens to be a treacherous and narrow passage near the tip of South America. Magellan's crew discovered this narrow passage in October 1520. The passage through the strait was fraught with challenges. They fought harsh weather conditions and even a mutiny, which Magellan suppressed, although tensions continued to increase among the crew.

After navigating this treacherous strait, Magellan and his fleet emerged into the Pacific Ocean. He named this body of water Mar

Pacifico due to its apparent tranquility compared to the stormy strait they had just passed through. However, this situation did not last. The crossing of the Pacific was perilous and prolonged, marked by extreme hardships that included the scarcity of food and fresh water. The crew had to resort to eating leather parts of their gear in order to survive.

Magellan's expedition eventually reached the Philippine archipelago. Magellan was killed in the Battle of Mactan in April 1521. The Battle of Mactan, fought on April 27th, was one of the first resistances against European colonization in Southeast Asia. A local chieftain, Lapu-Lapu, led the warriors of Mactan, an island, against Spanish forces under the command of Magellan. Magellan had attempted to coerce Lapu-Lapu to accept the authority of Rajah Humabon of Cebu, who had become an ally of the Spanish. Lapu-Lapu did not want to agree to such an arrangement.

While Magellan's forces had superior weaponry, they were significantly disadvantaged by the terrain and the unexpected tactical acumen of Lapu-Lapu's warriors. Magellan's men attempted to land on the shores of Mactan and found themselves trapped in the shallow waters, where their mobility was hindered by their heavy armor. Lapu-Lapu's forces exploited this. They quickly found weaknesses in the Spanish armor and focused their attack on the Spaniards' unprotected legs, using their spears, stones, and arrows very effectively.

The battle ended in Magellan's death. He was struck by a bamboo spear. The loss of Magellan was a significant setback for the Spanish and delayed further colonization efforts in the Philippines for decades. On the other hand, the event is celebrated in Philippine history as a symbol of resistance against foreign domination and has been immortalized in various cultural depictions and commemorations across the country.

The Search for the Northwest Passage and Its Challenges

The search for the Northwest Passage was another significant chapter in naval history. These explorers were driven by the desire to find a shorter trade route between Europe and Asia. This particular passage involved weaving through the Canadian Arctic Archipelago. This route was a potential economic boom but also posed considerable strategic and military implications.

Historically, the search for the Northwest Passage was fraught with peril. The harsh Arctic conditions posed significant challenges to any expedition. Many expeditions, such as those led by John Franklin in the 19th century, ended in tragedy, with ships icebound and men lost. The passage was so elusive that it took centuries of exploration.

From a naval perspective, the Northwest Passage held considerable strategic importance. This became especially so during the Cold War (1947-1991) after the passage was fully discovered in 1906. The passage became a critical route for military reinforcements and supply lines in the event of a Soviet attack. The Arctic's challenging conditions meant that those navigating the passage needed advanced naval technology and knowledge of Arctic environments.

Keys Expeditions in Search of the Northwest Passage

Henry Hudson

The Dutch East India Company sponsored a voyage for Henry Hudson in 1609 and again in 1610. He sought to explore North America's eastern seaboard and check out the Arctic's challenging environment. The lengthy and perilous journey around the Cape of Good Hope or through the Strait of Magellan was causing problems for seafarers.

Despite initial backing from English companies, Hudson shifted his allegiance to the Dutch because of their interest in discovering a faster route to Asia. In 1609, Hudson began his first and most famous voyage aboard the *Halve Maen* (*Half Moon*). His contract with the Dutch East India Company explicitly directed him to find the Northeast Passage near Novaya Zemlya (an archipelago in northern Russia). However, adverse conditions led him to sail westward toward North America instead. This decision was driven by his belief and possibly influenced by his communication with John Smith that a northwest passage to the Pacific could be found in the New World.

When he reached the New World, Hudson navigated along the Atlantic coast and eventually sailed up the river that would later bear his name, the Hudson River. His expedition reached as far as present-day Albany, New York. This exploration led the Dutch to lay claim to the region even though Hudson found that the river did not provide the passage to the Pacific that he had hoped for.

His final voyage in 1610 again sought the elusive Northwest Passage through what is now known as the Hudson Strait and into the vast Hudson Bay. The expedition faced extreme hardships. The men endured harsh winters and bouts of scurvy. These hardships led to increased tensions, culminating in a mutiny in June 1611. This mutiny resulted in Hudson, his teenage son John, and several other crew members being cast adrift in a small boat. They were never seen again. The fate of Hudson and these crew members remains one of the most enduring mysteries of early North American explorations.

Sir John Franklin

Sir John Franklin led the 1845 Franklin expedition, which aimed to chart the Northwest Passage. This expedition ended up being one of the most notorious tragedies in the history of polar exploration. Franklin and his 128 men set out with two ships, HMS *Erebus* and HMS *Terror*, both of which were lost in the Arctic ice.

The expedition was well equipped. Their ships were reinforced with steam engines and supplied with provisions for several years. However, by September 1846, the ships became trapped in the ice off King William Island. The situation quickly deteriorated. Franklin himself died in June 1847, and the crew attempted to escape overland to the mainland. Unfortunately, most perished from starvation, exposure, or lead poisoning, which was believed to have been caused by the canned food supplies.

Later searches led to the discovery of some of the crew's remains and belongings. All of these finds indicated desperate circumstances, including evidence of cannibalism among the crew as they attempted to survive. The local Inuit provided accounts and artifacts that helped piece together the grim details of the crew's fate.

The wrecks of the *Erebus* and *Terror* were finally located in 2014 and 2016. The wrecks offered new insights into the last days of the expedition.

Roald Amundsen

Roald Amundsen finally successfully navigated the Northwest Passage between 1903 and 1906. His expedition set sail aboard a small ship, the *Gjøa*, which proved the existence of a navigable route linking the Atlantic and Pacific Oceans through the Arctic archipelago of northern Canada.

The expedition set out from Oslo and rounded the southern tip of Greenland. From there, they followed a route that led them through

Baffin Bay and across the top of Canada from east to west. They spent the winters in the Arctic, using this time to conduct important scientific work that included magnetic observations. The harsh Arctic conditions required them to be careful when it came to handling their ship, and Amundsen's leadership and navigational skills were key to their survival and success.

One of the most significant aspects of this expedition was their successful engagement with the Inuit people. Amundsen learned survival techniques from them, such as using animal skins for warmth. This successful cultural exchange was instrumental in the success of this voyage. The Inuit were skilled seafarers themselves and were much better at navigating the cold climate.

In August 1905, the ship finally navigated the treacherous waters of the Northwest Passage and encountered a whaling ship from the Pacific Ocean. This was a clear sign that they had finally achieved their goal. The route they chartered was too shallow for commercial vessels, but their journey, ending in 1906, marked the first complete boat passage through the Northwest Passage and opened up a world of new possibilities for Arctic navigation.

The Consequences of Naval Exploration

The Age of Exploration might not have led specifically to naval warfare, but it profoundly shaped history, particularly through the establishment of trade networks and the expansion of colonial empires.

Naval exploration initiated by the European powers in the late 15th century connected disparate parts of the world into a global trading system. European explorers charted new territories and established new maritime routes. This new network facilitated the exchange of goods, ideas, and cultures across continents that were previously isolated from each other. These trade routes across the Atlantic and into the Indian and Pacific Oceans transformed local economies into integral parts of a global trade network. However, the exchange of commodities like spices, gold, and other valuable goods caused tensions among locals and other European powers.

Maritime prowess allowed European countries to project their power across vast distances and control strategic ports and waterways. They established colonies in the Americas, Africa, and Asia. The control of maritime routes and naval strength was directly linked to an empire's ability to administer and expand its territories. Naval dominance enabled countries like Britain and Spain to claim vast territories and maintain and defend these territories against rival powers and local resistance.

Naval exploration and the subsequent colonial conquest also had significant socioeconomic impacts on the colonized regions. The establishment of these colonies led to the creation of new social hierarchies and economic structures that were geared primarily toward benefiting the colonial powers. This often resulted in the exploitation of local populations and resources.

The use of naval capabilities in these explorations also introduced complex international relations and conflicts, which were often resolved through displays of naval strength. It influenced treaties and alliances that have had a long-lasting impact on international relations.

The historical consequences of these explorations and the use of naval power in colonialism have shaped the modern geopolitical and economic world map. The legacy of these maritime empires continues to influence global trade, politics, and cultural exchanges to this day.

Chapter 6 – The Line of Battle and Naval Tactics

Naval warfare in the Age of Sail was defined by the evolution of ship armaments and designs, resulting in the formidable concept of the line of battle. Naval tactics became more dynamic during this period, and galleons transformed and transitioned into ships of the line.

From Galleons to Ships of the Line: The Arms Race at Sea

The transition from galleons to ships of the line represented a seismic shift in naval warfare. This transition was underpinned by a relentless arms race that reshaped the geopolitical landscape of the time. Galleons had graceful lines that supported their stronger reliance on maneuverability and had been the workhorses of maritime exploration and conquests of the previous era. However, they proved to be limited, and this became more apparent as naval engagements grew in scale and intensity.

Ships of the line emerged as the answer to the shortcomings of galleons. These behemoths of the sea were characterized by their massive size and unparalleled firepower. Unlike their predecessors, ships of the line were floating fortresses that were capable of delivering devastating broadsides that could turn the tide of battle.

Construction of Ships of the Line

Ships of the line were monumental feats of engineering. Unlike previous generations, they were designed specifically to withstand the rigors of naval warfare while also being a noticeable representation of a nation's power floating on the ocean. The construction of these ships was a labor-intensive endeavor that demanded the combined expertise of shipwrights, carpenters, and artisans.

Saint-Esprit, a ship of the line in the French Navy.

    The hull of a ship of the line was typically constructed from sturdy oak timbers. Each of these timbers was carefully selected for their strength and durability. The shape of the hull was optimized for stability and seaworthiness. The keel was more pronounced, and a broad beam was used to support the weight of the heavy artillery and also provide stability during combat.

The ships of the line were among the largest vessels of their time. Most of them measured upward of one hundred feet in length and displaced thousands of tons of water. Their massive size allowed for the inclusion of extensive gun decks, crew quarters, and storage spaces. They also allowed for the installation of multiple tiers of cannons.

At the heart of every ship of the line were its cannons. These cannons were meticulously arranged along the gun decks so they could deliver devastating broadsides on their enemies. These cannons could range in caliber from 6-pounders to the imposing 32-pounders. Each of these was carefully positioned in order to maximize their firepower while also maintaining the ship's structural integrity. How many guns and how they were configured varied depending on the size and class of the vessel. The larger ships were capable of boasting over one hundred guns or more.

These ships were still reliant on wind power. This required an advanced rigging system that was composed of multiple masts, yards, and sails that allowed these vessels to harness the wind with precision. This complicated sail system enabled the ship to maneuver effectively in battle. Its rigging was meticulously maintained and was constantly adjusted by skilled sailors to optimize its speed and agility during combat.

Ships of the line served as symbols of national prestige and power. As such, the construction and commissioning of these formidable warships were often accompanied by grand ceremonies and celebrations.

You may think that their massive size and firepower diminished their maneuverability, but that was not the case. They were surprisingly versatile in battle. Skilled captains and crews employed a variety of tactical maneuvers, including line abreast formations, crossing the T, and feigned retreats, to outmaneuver and outgun their opponents. However, these tactics required precise coordination, discipline, and a deep understanding of naval strategy and seamanship among the crew.

The emergence of the ships of the line sparked feverish competition among maritime powers. They were all eager to assert their own dominance on the high seas. These powerful nations raced to outdo one another in constructing ever larger and more heavily armed vessels. Everyone was trying to achieve naval supremacy.

The relentless pursuit of superior armaments truly defined the arms race of this era. These nations invested heavily in the development of cutting-edge naval artillery. They poured an incredible amount of resources into the research and refinement of cannon technology. This drove innovation in metallurgy, ballistics, and gun carriage design that led to significant advancements in firepower and range.

The Line of Battle Tactic

The line of battle formation involved aligning warships in a single line, usually parallel to the enemy fleet. The primary goal of this tactic was to maximize the offensive capabilities of the broadside cannons while also maintaining order and minimizing risks like friendly fire or navigational confusion.

The ships of the line were organized based on their firepower, size, and role within the fleet. The larger and more heavily armed ships usually occupied the center of the line. Here, they could engage the strongest part of the enemy fleet while the lighter, faster ships were positioned on the flanks.

This tactic was designed to leverage concentrated broadside attacks. In this formation, the ships could fire all their guns from one side of the ship simultaneously. The formation helped to maintain a disciplined and cohesive fleet structure that enabled admirals to command their ships more effectively, even in the chaos of battle.

The formation also provided strategic defensive benefits. It created a solid battle line that could protect the more vulnerable ships and restrict the maneuvering capabilities of their enemies. All of this was crucial in dictating the terms of engagement, and it often forced the enemy to attack under less favorable conditions.

Key Naval Battles Using the Line of Battle Tactic

The Battle of Gabbard (1653)

The Battle of the Gabbard was fought on June 2nd and 3rd, 1653. This was during the First Anglo-Dutch War. This battle was a significant naval conflict near the Gabbard Shoal off Suffolk, England. It is noted for the strategic use of the line of battle tactic by the English fleet, which was able to secure a victory against the Dutch.

The conflict started with escalating trade tensions between England and the Dutch Republic. This was only exacerbated by the English

Navigation Act of 1651, which aimed to curb Dutch dominance in global trade. The failure of diplomatic efforts led to the outbreak of war in 1652.

Commanded at sea by generals George Monck and Richard Deane, who were later joined by Admiral Robert Blake and Admiral William Penn, the English fleet was composed of one hundred ships that included five fire ships. Fire ships were created from old or expendable ships filled with flammable materials like pitch, tar, and gunpowder. These ships were intentionally set on fire and sent toward enemy fleets to burn or destroy them. They often caused mass panic and broke enemy formations.

The Dutch, under Lieutenant Admiral Maarten Tromp, countered with ninety-eight ships and six fire ships. The English ships managed a strategic position in three squadrons, which allowed them to execute continuous broadsides that very quickly overwhelmed the Dutch fleet.

On the first day of battle, Tromp boldly attempted to board Admiral William Penn's flagship but was easily repelled. Subsequently, the English counterattacked. By the second day, the Dutch formation had broken, leading to their retreat and leaving the English in control of the seas.

The victory at Gabbard was key, as it allowed the English to establish a blockade that led to significant Dutch losses and eventually influenced the war's outcome. Using the line of battle tactic, the English could showcase their naval capabilities. The battle also highlighted the importance of making coordinated maneuvers and combining them with firepower.

The Four Days' Battle (1666)

The Four Days' Battle of 1666 was fought during the Second Anglo-Dutch War from June 1st to June 4th. It was one of the most prolonged and intense naval engagements of the Age of Sail. The battle occurred amidst escalating tensions and competition for maritime dominance between England and the Dutch Republic yet again. Both nations, as in the past, had heavily invested in their navies. The English were equipped with a more structured signaling system than the Dutch but faced challenges in coordination and maneuverability due to the size and complexity of their fleet formations.

The English used a flag signaling system. Each flagship carried a set of flags with specific patterns and colors that conveyed commands to the rest of the fleet. They were easily able to communicate orders and coordinate the ships. The system relied on prearranged instructions that were detailed in signal books that were in the hands of the commanders.

This particular engagement began off the Flemish coast. The scale and ferocity of combat were incredible. The English were initially outnumbered due to a split in their forces based on incorrect intelligence about French naval movements. They engaged the Dutch, who were under the command of Michiel de Ruyter. This battle saw extensive use of line of battle tactics. Ships attempted to attain a disciplined formation that maximized their broadside firing capabilities while also protecting themselves from enemy fire.

During the four days, the fleets executed several maneuvers that tested their ability to maintain these formations under the stress of battle. The English and Dutch fleets exchanged heavy broadsides, which demonstrated both the potential and limitations of the line of battle tactic. The Dutch managed to capitalize on their cohesive maneuvers and inflicted significant damage on the English fleet by the end of the fourth day.

This battle underscored the importance of effective signaling and command within the line of battle formation. The English struggled with their fleet coordination during the battle, which led to the development of more advanced signaling systems. These systems would later become crucial to the operational success of naval fleets in conflicts. The experience gained from this prolonged and chaotic battle also led naval tacticians to refine their strategies and emphasize the need for flexibility and responsiveness when it came to handling the fleet.

The Battle of Quiberon Bay (1759)

The Battle of Quiberon Bay was fought on November 20th, 1759, and was a critical moment of the Seven Years' War. This particular battle is often referred to as the "Trafalgar of the Seven Years' War" due to its decisive nature and the impact it had on naval dominance.[i] It took place off the coast of France near Saint Nazaire in Quiberon Bay and was instrumental in preventing the planned French invasion of Britain.

The French had assembled an invasion force in Brittany. They planned to escort it with a fleet from Brest into Britain. However, the British were aware of these plans and maintained a strict blockade of the

---

[i] This name was ascribed to it later; the Battle of Trafalgar took place in 1805.

French coast. In November 1759, the French fleet, led by Admiral Conflans, managed to escape the blockade during a storm. Admiral Sir Edward Hawke commanded the British fleet and pursued the French into Quiberon Bay despite the dangerous weather conditions and the hazardous rocky coastline.

These aggressive tactics paid off spectacularly. As the French fleet sought refuge in the bay, thinking the British would not dare to follow them into such treacherous waters, Hawke pressed the attack. The battle unfolded with ferocity, even with the challenging weather and shoals. The British sank several ships, including the *Thésée* and *Superbe*, while other members of the French fleet, including their flagship, *Soleil Royal*, ran aground and were destroyed or captured in the ensuing melee.

The Battle of Quiberon Bay ended any immediate threat of a French invasion while simultaneously weakening French naval power and advancing British control of the seas. This victory impacted French colonial ambitions while also securing British interests across the world. The battle also served to showcase the effectiveness of line of battle tactics in confining and decimating an enemy fleet within a restricted area.

The Battle of Quiberon Bay became a symbol of British naval prowess that stands up there with the later Battle of Trafalgar. You can hear this battle celebrated in the naval song "Heart of Oak" and see it commemorated in various paintings and accounts of the era.

Detailed Analysis of Naval Tactics at the Battle of Trafalgar (1805)

Admiral Horatio Nelson's strategy at Trafalgar broke from the traditional naval engagement tactics of using parallel lines. Surprisingly, these parallel line battles often resulted in inconclusive outcomes. Instead, Nelson's fleet was split into two columns and directed to attack the Franco-Spanish fleet perpendicularly. The Battle of Trafalgar, which took place on October 21st, 1805, was a landmark event in naval history and showcased Admiral Nelson's mastery of naval tactics, especially his deviation from conventional naval strategies.

In this particular battle, we find a strategic shift from the line of battle tactics to something more dynamic and decisive that could break the enemy's unity and morale. Nelson's maneuver at Trafalgar aimed to cut the enemy's line in two strategic places. The idea was to isolate and overwhelm sections of the enemy fleet to make them easier to defeat. This formation became known as cutting the line. The maneuver was risky and exposed the British ships to broadsides as they breached the enemy line, but at the same time, the tactic was designed to quickly sow chaos and disarray among the enemy, making it difficult for them to mount a coordinated response.

As the British columns approached the Franco-Spanish line, they faced heavy and devastating cannon fire. Leading the charge were the **HMS** *Victory* and **HMS** *Royal Sovereign*, which broke through the line, exposing themselves to intense broadsides. However, the British ships were able to maintain cohesion and exploit the new gaps in their enemy's lines. Nelson's tactic of "crossing the T" allowed the British to maximize their firepower by firing broadsides while the enemy could only use their forward and rear guns in response.

The British advantage was not only tactical but also technological. British ships were equipped with gun locks, which allowed for faster and more reliable firing. Gun locks were similar to the flintlock mechanism on a musket. Gunners could now fire the cannon exactly when they wanted instead of relying on slow-burning matches or fuses. The British also used carronades, short-range but powerful cannons that proved devastating at close range. These technological advances were complemented by a high level of training and discipline among British crews. These crews were able to reload and fire more rapidly than their adversaries and deliver more effective volleys. As such, the British were able to dominate the battle.

Nelson's leadership was instrumental in this victory. His aggressive strategies and his personal bravery (he led from the front in the **HMS** *Victory*) were pivotal to his success. His engagement style, encouraging close combat and boarding actions, favored the British sailors' superior seamanship and fighting spirit. His famous line, "England expects that every man will do his duty," exemplifies his ability to inspire his men to fight with the utmost courage and dedication. This gave the British a significant psychological edge. British morale was high, which improved their effectiveness in combat.

The Battle of Trafalgar resulted in a catastrophic defeat for the Franco-Spanish fleet. They lost twenty-two ships; the British lost none. However, the British lost many sailors, including Admiral Nelson. In total, the French and Spanish lost around 4,400 lives, 2,500 wounded, and over 7,000 captured. British numbers are estimated to be much less, with around 460 sailors killed and 1,200 wounded. The victory at Trafalgar ended any immediate threat of a Napoleonic invasion of Britain and also confirmed British naval supremacy. This supremacy would last for more than a century.

The Dominance of the Royal Navy

Between the 16th and the mid-19th century, the era commonly called the Age of Sail, the dominance of the Royal Navy had far-reaching global implications, affecting trade, colonization, and military strategy. The dominance of the Royal Navy continued past the Age of Sail, well into the 20th century.

The British Royal Navy controlled the seas. This allowed Britain to establish and maintain colonies across several continents. By the 19th century, its navy had evolved into the world's most formidable maritime force. It had to in order to support and sustain the empire's status as a predominant global power.

Since trade was the lifeblood of the British Empire, naval supremacy ensured the protection and control of vital trade routes across the Atlantic, into the Caribbean, across the Indian Ocean, and through to the Far East. The Royal Navy protected merchant ships from pirates and rival nations. It was their job to ensure the safe and profitable exchange of goods, ranging from spices and textiles to gold and silver. The Royal Navy was fully capable of enforcing blockades and controlling maritime traffic, which was a significant factor in economic warfare. These tactics were often used to weaken enemies by cutting off trade.

The Royal Navy also played a pivotal role in Britain's ability to colonize distant lands. Naval vessels didn't only transport settlers and troops. They also provided the necessary firepower to conquer and secure new territories. Naval forces were critical in battles that were started to acquire strategic ports and territories. These later became the basis for further expansion and points of control within the empire. The navy enabled Britain to establish a presence on every continent (except for Antarctica) and administer vast territories.

Chapter 7 – The Ironclads and the Industrial Revolution

The next great change in naval warfare came with the Industrial Revolution in the 19th century when ships shifted from wooden sailing ships to ironclad steam-powered vessels. Initially, these steam engines supplemented sail power before eventually replacing it entirely. This change allowed ships to navigate independently of wind patterns and enhanced their tactical flexibility and operational range. Steam-powered ships could maintain consistent speeds and perform complex maneuvers, which proved particularly advantageous in combat situations.

Steam propulsion came into broader use following the newer introduction of the screw propeller. This screw propeller proved more efficient and less vulnerable to damage in combat than the paddle wheels that were initially used. As steam technology evolved, it increasingly influenced ship design and led to the development of entirely steam-powered fleets.

Early Developments

The *Gloire* was designed by Henri Dupuy de Lôme and combined a wooden hull with iron armor. The plates used for the iron armor were initially only about 4.7 inches thick and then backed with an impressive 17 inches of timber. This innovative design came with limitations. Its maximum practical speed was only around eleven knots, and it still relied on both sails and steam for propulsion.

British Response with HMS *Warrior*

Not to be outdone by the French, the British Royal Navy commissioned the construction of HMS *Warrior* in 1860. This ship was going to be faster, better armed, and better protected than the French *Gloire*. The HMS *Warrior* was designed by Isaac Watts and built by the Thames Ironworks and Shipbuilding Company. The *Warrior* featured a fully ironclad hull that sported four-and-a-half-inch-thick armor. At the time, this particular armor was practically invulnerable to the current ordinances. There were a variety of guns on board, and it was powered by a Penn horizontal trunk steam engine that was capable of generating 5,627 horsepower, which allowed it to reach speeds up to 14.1 knots.

Evolution to True Ironclads

The *Warrior* was designed for battle but also for speed and operational flexibility. The intent was that it would be able to outrun any potential adversary and simultaneously dictate the terms of engagement. The construction and operational success of the *Warrior* led to the rapid development of similar vessels and propelled the Royal Navy further into a position of dominance at sea.

Meanwhile, across the Atlantic, the American Civil War prompted further innovations in ironclad design. John Erickson's design featured an even more revolutionary design that included a low-profile revolving turret that housed two large cannons. This design minimized the ship's exposure to enemy fire while also maximizing its offensive capabilities. The *Monitor* debuted in 1862 during the Battle of Hampton Roads against the CSS *Virginia*. This encounter was the first engagement of ironclad ships.

The American Civil War and Naval Revolution

The historic clash between the ironclad warships USS *Monitor* and CSS *Virginia* (formerly USS *Merrimack*) took place on March 8th, 1862. This battle marked a turning point in naval warfare due to the deployment of ironclads, but it also significantly impacted the naval strategies of both the Union and the Confederacy during the US Civil War.

On the first day of battle, the CSS *Virginia*, which was equipped with iron plating and an iron ram, successfully attacked the Union's wooden ships. They sank the USS *Cumberland* and set the US *Congress* aflame. These aggressive actions demonstrated the effectiveness and potential of ironclad ships against traditional wooden vessels.

On the next day, the USS *Monitor* arrived on the scene. The *Monitor* featured a revolutionary design, such as the revolving gun turret that allowed it to fire in all directions. The encounter between the *Monitor* and the *Virginia* on March 9th was a grinding duel, and neither side achieved a decisive victory. The ironclads' cannonballs mostly bounced off of each other's armor, showcasing the limitations of naval artillery against reinforced iron hulls.

This battle had some serious strategic implications. Although the direct outcome remains inconclusive, the presence of the *Monitor* effectively neutralized the threat posed by the *Virginia*. The *Monitor* was able to maintain the integrity of the Union's naval blockade against the Confederacy, which was crucial in stifling Southern trade and weakening the Confederate war effort over time.

The Battle of Hampton Roads caught the attention of naval powers worldwide. It led to immediate and sweeping changes in naval construction in several countries. While some countries were still building wooden warships, many shifted their focus to ironclad warships.

The Siege of Charleston (1863)

The siege of Charleston during the American Civil War was not only a significant land campaign but also a naval one and lasted from July 1863 to February 1865. The city of Charleston, South Carolina, was a major Confederate port and hub for blockade running, which made it a crucial target for Union forces that sought to squeeze the Confederacy's resources and operational capabilities.

Charleston's defense was formidable and managed by skilled Confederate commanders like General P. G. T. Beauregard. The city held extensive coastal fortifications, floating mines, ironclad rams, and even the use of early submarines. Fort Sumter and Fort Wagner were central to these defenses, with Fort Sumter enduring prolonged bombardment but never being taken by force, even though it was eventually reduced to rubble.

On April 7th, 1863, the Union attacked. This marked one of the earliest assaults involving ironclads, and they faced heavy fire from Confederate batteries. This attack was a failure but showcased the challenges of overcoming fortified positions with naval bombardments alone.

The Confederate ironclads played a significant role even before the formal siege. In an audacious move on January 31st, 1863, the ironclads CSS *Palmetto State* and CSS *Chicora* launched a surprise attack on Union blockaders. This surprise attack only proved the potential impact of Confederate naval capabilities. Under cover of darkness and commanded by General P. G. T. Beauregard, the Confederate ironclads ventured into Charleston Harbor and launched a surprise attack on the Union wooden steamers. The *Palmetto State* rammed and disabled the USS *Mercedita*, which was then forced to surrender. The damage to the ship was bad enough that the crew thought they were sinking, although they never did. At the same time, the CSS *Chicora* engaged the USS *Keystone State* and inflicted severe damage with its heavy guns. This surprise attack briefly disrupted the Union blockade until the formal siege in July.

This use of ironclads demonstrated the potential and limitations of ironclad ships. They were slow and cumbersome ships because of their armored hulls and heavy armaments, but this also allowed them to challenge traditional wooden ships effectively since they were particularly vulnerable to their powerful artillery. The Confederates were able to use their ironclads strategically in their harbor defenses and against blockades, providing them with a brief success against superior forces and briefly lifting the blockade that had been imposed by the Union Navy.

Even after this encounter, the Confederate ironclads remained primarily defensive assets. They were used to safeguard the channels between Charleston Harbor forts against further Union naval incursions. The Union forces strengthened their blockade with more ironclads.

One of the most notable naval aspects of the siege was the use of the *H. L. Hunley*. The *Hunley* was the first combat submarine to successfully sink an enemy ship, in this case, the USS *Housatonic*, in February 1864. The concept of underwater navigation was not new; it dates back to antiquity with notable early attempts like the *Turtle* during the American Revolution. However, it wasn't until the Civil War, with the deployment of the *Huntley*, that submarines demonstrated their military potential by sinking an enemy ship.

The *H. L. Hunley* was developed as a part of the Confederacy's efforts to break the Union blockade that was choking the Southern states' ability to maintain the war effort. The submarine was privately built and engineered to attack by embedding a spar torpedo into the hull of enemy ships. Spar torpedoes were new weapons consisting of an explosive charge mounted on a long pole or spar. They were used to strike and detonate against an enemy ship's hull, usually below the waterline.

The *Hunley* approached the *Housatonic* off Charleston Harbor and successfully embedded its spar torpedo into the ship's hull. This caused significant damage and subsequently sunk the vessel. It is important to note that the *Hunley* was not fully submerged when it launched its attack. Also, despite the success, the *Hunley* and all eight crew members disappeared. The exact cause of the sinking remains a mystery, with stories full of speculation. The submarine was recovered in 2000 when it was raised from the ocean floor off Charleston. It currently rests at the Warren Lasch Conservation Center in Charleston, South Carolina.

The use of the *Hunley* inspired the later extensive use of submarines in both World War I and World War II, where they played a far more strategic and impactful role.

Other Ironclad Encounters

The Battle of Lissa (1866)

One of the most significant ironclad clashes after the American Civil War was the Battle of Lissa in 1866, which took place during the Third Italian War of Independence. This particular engagement occurred between the Austrian Empire and the Kingdom of Italy. It was one of the first major sea battles that involved ironclad warships. It also featured the use of ramming as a key tactic.

The Austrian fleet was commanded by Rear Admiral Wilhelm von Tegetthoff, who was outnumbered and outgunned by the Italian fleet under the command of Admiral Carlo di Persano. The Austrian fleet's strategy was to engage in close-quarter combat. This decision leveraged their ships' ability to ram their opponents as a means to compensate for their lesser firepower.

The Austrian fleet had fewer ironclads than the Italians, being outnumbered seven to twelve in that department. They decided to form their ships into a wedge formation with the intent to break through Italian lines and create confusion. Perhaps this decision followed the strategic decisions made by Nelson a few decades before.

The Italian fleet was technologically more advanced. However, it suffered from command and coordination issues. These issues were only exacerbated by Admiral Persano's last-minute decision to transfer his flag to another ship, which led to further disarray and a virtually ineffective command during the battle.

The Italian fleet was preparing for land operations against the island, so Tegetthoff seized the opportunity to attack. He drove his fleet in his wedge formation at the disorganized Italians, who were still struggling to line up. The Italians' confusion, combined with mixed signals and a lack of cohesive action, cost them significant time.

The Austrians' aggressive tactics paid off, as their ships managed to breach the Italian lines and engage in close-quarter combat. They were able to successfully use ramming tactics to their advantage. This particular battle saw heavy use of ramming combined with broadside exchanges, which were relatively new due to the ironclad's robust armor that traditional gunfire could not easily penetrate. The Battle of Lissa ended as a decisive victory for the Austrian fleet.

Naval Developments Post-Civil War

The period following the American Civil War saw an intense naval arms race among the world's major powers. The United States initiated a substantial naval construction program under President Grover Cleveland, which continued under his successors. America commissioned faster cruisers, armored cruisers, and the first American battleships, which propelled the US Navy into a major global force by the end of the 19th century. The European powers, notably Britain and Germany, were also inspired to expand and modernize their navies.

The technological leap in the US Navy between the mid-1880s and the mid-1890s was particularly intense. The US Navy transitioned from a relatively modest force to one of the world's leading navies. This change was supported by domestic industrial growth, which allowed for the in-house production of ship armor and heavy artillery that they previously had to source from Europe.

Advancements were also made in naval armament. The world saw the development of more powerful guns and the introduction of new weaponry like torpedoes and submarine technology, which continued to evolve well into the 20th century.

All of these developments and advancements set the stage for the naval strategies used in World War One, and they continue to influence naval thought and construction today. The intense naval arms races of the late 19th and early 20th centuries not only reshaped military strategies but also greatly impacted politics and the balance of power.

Chapter 8 – The World Wars and Naval Warfare

The onset of World War I marked a significant shift from the traditional battles of fleet engagements to a more nuanced and technologically driven form of warfare. The oceans became arenas where great powers clashed with devastating new tools of war: submarines that hid beneath the surface and battleships that ruled the waves with unmatched firepower.

These new types of conflicts tested the limits of human ingenuity and the technological prowess of the nations that were involved. From the depths of the sea to the vast expanses of the ocean, naval warfare not only determined the immediate outcomes of battles but also influenced the geopolitical landscape of the 20th century.

Submarine Warfare and the Blockade of Germany in World War I

Submarines became a very strategic tool during World War I. Germany faced a significant wall known as the British Royal Navy. The Germans deployed their U-boat fleet in a bid to disrupt Allied supply lines across the Atlantic. They wanted to sever Britain from its critical overseas resources, an endeavor that escalated with the adoption of unrestricted submarine warfare. Unrestricted submarine warfare meant German submarines would attack military and civilian vessels without warning. This move drastically intensified the war and drew previously neutral nations, most notably the United States, into the conflict. One of the reasons the US joined the war was the tragic sinking of the *Lusitania* in 1915, which resulted in a significant number of American casualties.

In response to the U-boat threat, Britain enforced a stringent naval blockade against Germany. It sought to intercept any imports essential for Germany's war efforts and civilian population. This blockade effectively throttled German access to vital resources and contributed to widespread hardship and unrest within Germany as the war continued to drag on.

The German U-boats were initially few in number and significantly disrupted Allied shipping. By 1917, the scale of destruction caused by these submarines had reached its peak, with hundreds of thousands of tons of Allied shipping sunk in just a few months. The British responded with the convoy system, which was groups of merchant ships escorted by armed ships, to mitigate Germany's U-boat effectiveness. While initially this system had its challenges, it eventually proved successful in reducing losses. However, U-boats continued to pose a formidable threat throughout the war.

By the end of the war, the U-boat campaigns had sunk thousands of ships and numerous submarines. Despite their failure to decisively defeat Britain, the U-boats had a profound impact on the war's naval strategies and the eventual entry of the United States into the conflict.

A U-boat at a memorial in Germany. [vi]

German U-boats

The U-boat, a shortened name of *Unterseeboots*, was part of a fleet of forty-eight submarines that varied in design and included both diesel and kerosene engines. Those designed with diesel engines would betray their position with their exhaust, a problem that was later mitigated by the development of more efficient diesel engines.

The German U-boats were organized into several classes, which included the UB and UC classes. These were smaller and more often used for mine-laying operations in coastal waters. By the end of World War One, Germany had produced 375 U-boats, which sunk over twelve million tons of Allied shipping. The success of the U-boats was even more profound when you consider the British countermeasures with convoys and Q-ships, which were camouflaged vessels that held concealed weaponry designed to lure and destroy U-boats.

The most notable U-boat was the SM *U-9*, commanded by Lieutenant Otto Weddigen. In a single daring operation in September 1914, *U-9* sank three British armored cruisers: the HMS *Aboukir*, HMS *Cressy*, and HMS *Hogue*. This attack shook British naval confidence and demonstrated the great threat these relatively small submarines posed.

British Q-Ships

British Q-ships, or mystery ships, were a unique and innovative naval strategy used during World War One. They were specifically designed to combat the threat of German U-boats. Essentially, these vessels were decoy ships. Outwardly, they appeared as ordinary merchant ships, but they were heavily armed with concealed weaponry. The idea was to lure U-boats into making surface attacks. When they rose to the surface, the Q-ship would reveal their hidden guns and engage the enemy submarines.

The concept of deception in naval warfare was not new; however, the implementation of Q-ships took this to a new level. They were fitted with false structures like fake funnels and hinged sides that could quickly be dropped to reveal the ship's armaments. The crews would perform "panic parties," where they pretended to abandon the ship to convince the U-boats that they were vulnerable merchant vessels. Once the U-boat came to the surface and into close range, the Q-ship would drop its disguise, raise the Royal Navy's white ensign, and open fire.

The Q-ships managed to sink or damage several U-boats. Their success was limited and quickly waned as the war progressed because the Germans became aware of these tactics. The inherent risk of operating Q-ships was that they had to allow U-boats to approach dangerously close before they could attack. By the end of the war, the secrecy that was vital to their success had diminished, so they were increasingly seen as less effective compared to other anti-submarine measures that were developed.

Dreadnoughts and Battlecruisers

Dreadnoughts and battlecruisers were the towering titans of naval warfare in the early 20th century. These ships were central to the naval strategies of the world's leading powers, most notably Britain and Germany, which engaged in a significant naval arms race prior to World War One. The HMS *Dreadnought*, launched in 1906, revolutionized naval warfare with its all-big-gun design (uniform large-caliber guns). It set a new standard that quickly made existing battleships obsolete and spurred similar constructions among other naval powers.

A dreadnought ship was revolutionary at the time with its large-caliber guns and steam turbine engines that allowed for speed. The older battleships had mixed-caliber weapons and slower propulsion. Eventually, the dreadnought dominated naval warfare and made the older battleships obsolete. The new battlecruisers were very similar to dreadnoughts but prioritized speed over armor. They were equipped with similar large caliber guns but used thinner armor to travel at higher speeds.

The growing anticipation of large-scale naval engagements involving these dreadnoughts shaped much of the pre-war naval buildup. Surprisingly, the expected decisive clashes of dreadnought fleets rarely materialized during the war. There was one primary exception: the Battle of Jutland in 1916, which was the largest naval battle of World War One. It involved a significant number of dreadnoughts and battlecruisers from both the British and German fleets.

The Royal Navy's HMS Dreadnought.[vii]

The Battle of Jutland (1916)

The Battle of Jutland was fought from May 31st to June 1st, 1916. It remains the largest naval battle of World War One and the only full-scale clash of battleships during the war. It involved the British Royal Navy's grand fleet under Admiral Sir John Jellicoe and the Imperial German Navy's High Seas Fleet under Vice Admiral Reinhard Scheer.

The German fleet was hoping to break the British blockade of Germany and also lure portions of the British fleet into a trap to destroy them completely. The British became aware of these German movements through communications they intercepted. So, they sought to engage and rout the High Seas Fleet. The battle occurred near Jutland, which was a strategic location off the coast of Denmark and involved about 250 ships and 100,000 men from both sides.

The battle began with a confrontation between the British battlecruiser force led by Vice Admiral David Beatty and the German scouting group under Franz Hipper. The British battlecruisers suffered heavy losses. This included a catastrophic explosion of the HMS *Queen Mary* and HMS *Invincible* due to direct hits to their ammunition magazines.

As the main fleets entered the battle, Jellicoe managed to position the Grand Fleet to his advantage, attempting to "cross the T" of the German fleet. (The Grand Fleet was the Royal Navy's main battle fleet during WWI. It consisted of dozens of dreadnoughts, battlecruisers, and support ships.) This was a strategic move dating back to the Age of Sail that allowed a line of ships to fire broadsides while the enemy could only use their forward guns. This was the exact move that Admiral Nelson used at Trafalgar. However, Scheer responded by executing a daring withdrawal in darkness and avoiding a decisive defeat. This maneuver spared the German fleet from complete destruction, but it also affirmed the strength and readiness of the Royal Navy, which continued to control the North Sea.

While this battle might remain inclusive, it reinforced British naval dominance and the effectiveness of the blockade against Germany. The heavy losses on both sides highlighted the deadly nature of modern naval warfare and the significant role of battleships and fleet actions. The Germans learned that the British fleet was formidable and refrained from further large-scale naval engagements for the remainder of the war. Instead, they shifted their focus to submarine warfare.

Other Notable Naval Battles of WWI

Battle of Heligoland Bight (August 1914)

The first significant naval engagement of World War One between British and German naval forces occurred on August 28th, 1914. This particular battle marked the beginning of naval confrontations in the North Sea and is notable because of the boldness of the British attack on German patrols near their own bases.

Commodore Reginald Tyrwhitt led the British with the aid of Commodore Roger Keyes. Together, they sought to challenge German naval patrols close to Heligoland Bight. This particular area was important because it was the main exit for the Imperial German Navy into the North Sea. The British naval forces included destroyers and submarines, which were strategically positioned to intercept and ambush any returning German destroyers at dawn.

The German Navy was not expecting a direct confrontation so close to their bases. The British tactic was aggressive and well coordinated, and the Germans suffered greatly. The battle escalated when British battlecruisers, commanded by Admiral David Beatty, and additional forces joined the fray. The British successfully engaged several German light cruisers and destroyers, which resulted in the sinking of the German ships SMS *Ariadne*, SMS *Cöln*, and others.

The outcome of this particular encounter was a victory for the British. German casualties were significantly higher than those of the British. This success boosted British morale and confidence and forced the German High Seas Fleet to be more cautious in their operations. In fact, they kept mostly to port for quite some time after the battle.

Battle of Coronel (November 1914)

Off the coast of central Chile on November 1st, 1914, there was a significant naval engagement that resulted in a notable victory for the Imperial German Navy. Under Vice Admiral Graf Maximilian von Spee, a squadron known as the German East Asia Squadron encountered and decisively defeated a British squadron commanded by Rear Admiral Sir Christopher Craddock.

The German forces were comprised of the armored cruisers SMS *Scharnhorst* and SMS *Gneisenau*, which were supported by light cruisers SMS *Dresden*, SMS *Leipzig*, and SMS *Nurnberg*. The British squadron was smaller and less suited for battle. It consisted of the armored cruisers HMS *Good Hope* and HMS *Monmouth* and the light cruiser HMS *Glasgow*. Alongside them was an armed merchant cruiser, HMS *Otranto*. These British ships were older and less capable in a fight against the more modern and better-armed German vessels.

The battle began in the late afternoon and continued into the evening as the light faded. The German cruisers used their superior firepower and effective gunnery to quickly gain the upper hand. Both HMS *Good Hope* and HMS *Monmouth* were sunk during the battle with significant loss of life. There were no survivors from either of the British armored cruisers. In stark contrast, the German squadron suffered minimal casualties, with only a few wounded and no ships lost.

This victory at Coronel was a significant morale booster for Germany and a shock to Britain, which had not suffered a naval defeat like that in over a century.

Battle of the Falkland Islands (December 1914)

A little over a month after von Spee's forces won a victory at Coronel, they entered a decisive encounter against Vice Admiral Sir Doveton Sturdee of the British Royal Navy. Sturdee's forces overwhelmingly defeated Admiral Graf Maximilian von Spee's East Asia Squadron.

Following their victory at the Battle of Coronel, von Spee's squadron ventured into the South Atlantic to target the British coaling station at Port Stanley on the Falkland Islands. What he didn't know was that the British had already dispatched a powerful squadron to intercept him, including the battlecruisers HMS *Invincible* and HMS *Inflexible*.

As the German forces approached the Falklands, their lookouts caught sight of the masts of the British ships in the harbor. Spee realized he was facing a superior force and attempted to escape, but the British ships were faster and more heavily armored, and they quickly pursued the Germans. The resulting battle was one-sided. The German armored cruisers, along with other vessels in the squadron, were sunk. Admiral von Spee and many of his men went down with their ships. This battle not only avenged the British loss at Coronel but also removed a significant raiding threat from Germany's overseas naval forces.

After the Battle of the Falkland Islands, the majority of the Imperial German Navy was confined to the North Sea for the remainder of the war. The only German ship to escape the Falkland Islands was the light cruiser *Dresden*, which was later scuttled in March 1915.

Battle of Dogger Bank (January 1915)

The Battle of Dogger Bank occurred on January 24th, 1915, in the North Sea. This was another significant confrontation between British and German naval forces. This battle was primarily between British battlecruisers under Vice Admiral Sir David Beatty and a German squadron led by Rear Admiral Franz von Hipper.

The British had quite an advantage when it came to naval intelligence. They had intercepted and decoded German wireless transmissions that revealed Hipper's plan to launch a raid. This intelligence allowed David Beatty's forces to intercept the German squadron. The British fleet included the battlecruisers **HMS** *Lion*, **HMS** *Tiger*, **HMS** *Princess Royal*, **HMS** *New Zealand*, and **HMS** *Indomitable*.

The German squadron suffered significant damage, in particular, the armored cruiser **SMS** *Blücher*, which was sunk during the battle. Since the Germans suffered heavier casualties, it was claimed to be a British tactical victory. However, the battle exposed some weaknesses in British tactics and ship design. Their battlecruisers were far more vulnerable to heavy German fire than they had anticipated.

Even with these issues, the outcome of Dogger Bank boosted British morale and reinforced their control of the North Sea. Yet again, the

German fleet decided to adopt a more cautious approach in future operations.

The Interwar Period

Following World War I, the great powers wanted to design a way to prevent a naval arms race like the one that followed the American Civil War. The Washington Naval Treaty, which was signed in 1922, was initiated by US President Warren G. Harding. The treaty was a collective effort by the United States, the British Empire, Japan, France, and Italy in order to limit naval construction. It was a bid to maintain peace and save on national defense expenditures.

This treaty imposed strict limitations on battleship and battlecruiser tonnage and armaments. It set a tonnage ratio of 5:5:3 for capital ships (the largest and most powerful warships) between the US, Britain, and Japan. The treaty also placed caps on the size and armament of ships. These caps effectively halted the construction of new battleships for a decade and led to the scrapping of existing or planned vessels in order to adhere to the set quotas. It also placed restrictions on fortifications in the Pacific. This aimed to stabilize the region by maintaining the status quo among the competing powers.

Initially, this treaty was successful in slowing the naval arms race and reducing military spending, but it had its limitations. For one, it failed to cover all types of naval vessels like cruisers, destroyers, and submarines, which led to competition in these arenas. The treaty's restrictions were also eventually evaluated and perceived to be too restrictive by Japan and other nations, which led to rising militarism and the eventual breakdown of these agreements in the 1930s. At that point, nations began to rearm and expand their fleets.

Advances in Aircraft Carrier Design and Naval Aviation

Alongside this arms limitation treaty and its discussions, advancements were made in aircraft carrier design and naval aviation. The limitations placed on battleship and battlecruiser construction by the Washington Naval Treaty indirectly promoted the development of aircraft carriers to the point where several capital ships under construction were converted into aircraft carriers. The most notable of these were the American ships *Lexington* and *Saratoga* and the Japanese ship *Akagi*.

The US and Britain were able to maintain substantial tonnages in aircraft carriers and still follow the treaty's terms, which facilitated the growth of carrier fleets. The design of carriers evolved rapidly as well. They enhanced the launch and recovery mechanisms and increased the size and effectiveness of the air wings they could support. Greater focus was placed on carrier-based operations, which would come to dominate naval strategy during World War II.

World War II

The attack on Pearl Harbor on December 7th, 1941, was a meticulously planned surprise strike by the Japanese Imperial Navy Air Service. This surprise attack was against the US naval base at Pearl Harbor, Hawaii, and its devastating results led directly to America's entry into World War Two. Japan's desire was to neutralize the US Pacific fleet as a means to prevent American interference with Japan's plans to expand its influence in Southeast Asia.

The attack commenced at 7:48 a.m. and involved two waves of Japanese aircraft. These waves totaled 353 planes, and they took off from six aircraft carriers, which was a decided change in naval warfare from previous encounters. The Japanese targeted the battleships, aircraft, and naval installations at Pearl Harbor. The USS *Arizona* and the USS *Oklahoma* were among the eight battleships that were either sunk or severely damaged. The USS *Arizona* suffered a catastrophic explosion when a bomb penetrated its forward ammunition magazine. This explosion resulted in the loss of over one thousand crew members.

The attack did not strike the American aircraft carriers. Luckily, they were not present at the base during the attack. This oversight would prove to be a significant tactical blunder for Japan because these carriers played a crucial role in the US naval response. Key facilities like oil storage depots, shipyards, and submarine docks were also left largely intact. This allowed the US Navy to recover more quickly than might have otherwise been possible.

The immediate consequence of this naval encounter was the US declaration of war against Japan the following day. This marked America's official entry into World War II. The attack on Pearl Harbor has since remained a seminal moment in American history.

The Battle of Midway (1942)

The Battle of Midway took place from June 3rd to June 6th, 1942 in the Pacific theater. It marked the first major victory for the United States against Japan and is considered one of the most decisive battles in naval history due to its strategic implications.

The battle began with the United States gaining crucial intelligence from decrypted Japanese messages. These messages revealed Japan's strategy and timing for the attack on Midway Atoll. The US Navy, under Admiral Chester Nimitz, Frank Jack Fletcher, and Raymond Spruance, used this information to prepare an ambush. Admiral Chuichi Nagumo led the Japanese fleet and aimed to extend its defensive perimeter by capturing the Midway Atoll and using it as a base to launch further operations. These operations could even potentially reach Hawaii.

On the morning of June 4th, Japanese aircraft bombed Midway Island but did not achieve their goal, which was to significantly degrade the island's defensive capabilities. Meanwhile, the US Navy aircraft from the carriers USS *Enterprise*, USS *Hornet*, and USS *Yorktown* launched attacks against the Japanese carrier fleet. Despite heavy losses among the first wave of the US torpedo bombers, subsequent waves of US dive bombers caught the Japanese carriers *Akagi*, *Kaga*, *Soryu*, and *Hiryu* off-guard. The US bombers were able to deliver devastating blows that would ultimately sink these ships.

The loss of four frontline aircraft carriers and many of its most experienced pilots weakened the Japanese fleet and began a shift in the balance of naval power in the Pacific to the United States. This US victory halted Japanese expansion in the Pacific and initiated a series of US offensive operations. They were able to push Japan into a defensive posture for the remainder of the war.

The Battle of Midway is noted for the incredible odds the US forces had to overcome and the high stakes involved. It was a battle where the opposing fleets never saw each other directly. The outcome was largely determined by air attacks launched from naval carriers. This was a new form of naval warfare that emphasized the importance of aircraft carriers over battleships.

The Battle of the Atlantic

The Battle of the Atlantic was a long engagement that spanned from 1939 to 1945. It was the longest continuous military campaign of World War II and was crucial in determining the overall success of the Allied forces. It primarily revolved around the Allied efforts to protect transatlantic shipping against the formidable threat posed, once again, by German U-boats. The U-boats focused on severing Britain's vital supply lines.

The German strategy was to rely heavily on U-boat wolfpacks (groups of U-boats) to attack and sink merchant convoys in the Atlantic. The strategy did not change much from World War I, as they still aimed to starve Britain into submission. At its peak, this campaign threatened to overwhelm the Allies, with Adolf Hitler making offers to Britain to surrender. Britain considered it because the British had already suffered significant losses of ships and essential supplies, as well as continuous air raid bombings on large cities like London. However, several critical developments shifted the balance of power. Allied cryptanalysts, building on early Polish successes in breaking the Enigma cipher, managed to decrypt key German communications. This intelligence breakthrough allowed the Allies to reroute convoys away from these U-boat wolfpacks while simultaneously directing anti-submarine forces more effectively.

The British once again used the convoy system. They grouped ships together and provided them with armed naval escorts, which allowed the Allies to significantly reduce their losses. The system was enhanced by the development and deployment of long-range aircraft and escort carriers.

Technological advancements like improved sonar, radar, and the development of depth charges played crucial roles in detecting and attacking U-boats before they could strike. The Allies also increased the production of ships, particularly in the United States. This increased production helped to replace losses and maintain critical supply lines. Over time, all of these measures effectively neutralized the U-boat threat, culminating in what was known as Black May in 1943, when the Germans suffered such heavy losses that they were forced to retreat from their positions in the North Atlantic.

Black May (1943)

By May 1943, the cumulative efforts of the Allies, which had been enhanced by technological advances and improved tactics, began to take a devastating toll on the German U-boats. Additionally, the operational range of air cover was extended with the introduction of very long range (VLR) aircraft like the B24 Liberator. These aircraft, alongside escort carriers, helped to close the mid-Atlantic gap where U-boats had previously operated without much opposition. This enhanced air coverage proved instrumental in sinking or damaging U-boats that had surfaced to attack or recharge their batteries.

During Black May, the Allies sank forty-one German U-boats, which represented a significant percentage of the operational U-boat fleet. The heavy losses were unsustainable for the German Kriegsmarine (Nazi Germany's navy) and Admiral Karl Dönitz, the commander of the U-boat forces. He withdrew his remaining U-boats from the North Atlantic. This marked the end of what had been an effective offensive strategy against Allied shipping. The Allies were now able to build up more military forces in preparation for invasions like D-Day.

Churchill and His Special Operations Executive (SOE)

Throughout the conflict, British Prime Minister Winston Churchill was deeply involved in the strategic decisions of the Battle of the Atlantic. He recognized the critical importance of maintaining Britain's supply lines and advocated strongly for the resources needed to combat the U-boat menace. He did this even at the expense of other military priorities. He also understood that it was highly unlikely the US would join the war without safe passage across the Atlantic. Churchill's leadership was instrumental in prioritizing and coordinating the multifaceted approach that ultimately secured the Atlantic shipping lanes. With his papers being released in 2016, we have a far deeper understanding of the lengths Churchill went to in order to rid the Atlantic of U-boat threats.

Churchill initiated daring special operations like Operation Postmaster to take back the Atlantic. In January 1942, a small-scale raiding force, along with the Special Operations Executive (SOE) carried out a mission with the primary objective of seizing three Axis vessels anchored in the neutral harbor of Santa Isabel on the Spanish island of Fernando Poe (now Bioko) without provoking Spain into joining the Axis forces.

This operation targeted the Italian merchant vessel *Duchessa d'Aosta*, a large German tug called *Likomba*, and a diesel-powered barge named *Bibundi*. The secret naval plan was executed under cover of darkness to maintain plausible deniability and avoid any direct links to the British government. The aim was to make it appear as if the act could have been carried out by pirates.

The operation was executed flawlessly. This small British force managed to board and commandeer the ships and navigate them out of the harbor without any casualties. This feat was accomplished through a combination of stealth, precise timing, and the element of surprise. Other distractions, such as a dinner party arranged for the ship's officers to keep them away from their posts during the operation, were also used. The importance of this mission was that the merchant vessel was a listening ship, serving as a spy for Axis powers to gain information about Allied shipping movements. The mission successfully disrupted access to maritime activities and secured valuable naval assets for the Allies.

The captured ships were repurposed and used for Allied purposes. The Allies' careful planning and execution were successful in not pushing Spain to alter its stance in the war. This operation directly contributed to the resulting end of the U-boat threat.

Chapter 9 – The Cold War and Nuclear Navies

The development of nuclear-powered submarines changed the strategic landscape profoundly. Unlike their diesel-electric predecessors, nuclear submarines could stay submerged for extended periods; they were only limited by the crew's endurance and food supplies.

This was all part of the Cold War (1947-1991). While labeled a "war," it was more a period of intense political, ideological, and military rivalry between the United States and the Soviet Union (and their respective allies). In the simplest terms, it was a struggle between capitalism and communism, but it never escalated to direct military conflict. The Cold War involved proxy wars, nuclear arms and space races, and global influence campaigns.

The USS *Nautilus*

The USS *Nautilus* was commissioned in 1954. It was the first operational nuclear-powered submarine. This particular ship was powered by the Submarine Thermal Reactor (STR), which was later redesignated as the S2W reactor. This was a pressurized water reactor that was developed by the Westinghouse Electric Corporation and Bettis Atomic Power Laboratory. This pioneering design became the basis for nearly all subsequent US nuclear-powered submarines and surface combat ships.

The *Nautilus*'s operational debut showcased the advantages of nuclear propulsion. It was submerged for a trip from New London, Connecticut, to Puerto Rico, covering 1,200 nautical miles in less than 90 hours without surfacing. This was the longest submerged cruise by a submarine at the highest sustained speed at that time. This capability to remain submerged for extended periods without the need for air rendered traditional anti-submarine warfare methods like radar and aircraft effectively obsolete.

In 1958, the *Nautilus* achieved another historic milestone. It completed the first voyage under the geographic North Pole. This operation demonstrated its capabilities in extreme conditions but also had strategic implications for the Cold War period. It showcased the potential of nuclear-powered submarines to execute missions in previously inaccessible parts of the world.

While these were impressive achievements, the USS *Nautilus* had its share of design and operational challenges. The German Type XXI submarine (or U-boat) inspired its design, but it was not optimized for the potential speeds nuclear power could achieve. The submarine also experienced issues like significant vibrations at higher speeds that impacted the use of its sonar systems.

Nuclear Deterrence and the Balance of Power at Sea

The introduction of nuclear-powered ballistic missile submarines (SSBNs) during the Cold War fundamentally transformed the strategies of nuclear deterrence and significantly altered the global balance of power. The deployment of these submarines by both the United States and the Soviet Union provided each with a formidable and survivable second-strike capability, which became central to most military doctrines.

The USS *George Washington* was commissioned in 1960 and was the first operational SSBN in the US Navy. It was equipped with Polaris ballistic missiles. This capability allowed it to conduct extended submerged patrols while remaining undetected for prolonged periods. This ensured that it was a continuous at-sea deterrent. The accompanying US strategy emphasized the importance of a triad system that comprised long-range bombers, intercontinental ballistic missiles (ICBMs), and sea-launched ballistic missiles (SLBMs) to maintain a credible threat of retaliation. This was designed to prevent a nuclear attack by ensuring there would be mutually assured destruction (MAD).

On the other side of the conflict, the Soviet Union recognized the strategic use of SSBNs and worked rapidly to match and even counterbalance US capabilities. Their first SSBN, the *K-19*, was launched in the same year as the USS *George Washington*. The Soviet Union's strategy during the Cold War was to construct a significant number of nuclear submarines. Estimations account for the commission of around five to ten nuclear submarines annually at the height of the Cold War. By the late 1990s, the Soviet Union, and then later Russia, had constructed a total of 245 nuclear submarines. This was more than all other nations combined.

The presence of SSBNs contributed to a shift in strategic military planning. Both superpowers had the capability to launch nuclear missiles from hidden locations anywhere in the world's oceans. This capability increased the lethality and unpredictability of nuclear forces and made traditional notions of front lines and geographic buffers obsolete. Neither side could strike without facing inevitable and severe retaliation from the other.

The Cold War and Naval Standoffs

The pinnacle of the Cold War, the Cuban missile crisis of October 1962, clearly illustrates the dramatic and dangerous role of naval power in international diplomacy. American reconnaissance discovered there were Soviet missile installations in Cuba. This discovery prompted President John F. Kennedy to implement a naval blockade, which the US government termed a quarantine, to prevent further military supplies from reaching the island. This blockade was crucial in preventing a potential nuclear confrontation. It also showed how much the US Navy played a strategic role in enforcing international peace and security during a critical time of the Cold War.

Kennedy's decision to use a naval blockade instead of immediate military strikes was important in maintaining control over the escalation of the crisis. The blockade effectively prevented any additional missiles and military equipment from being delivered to Cuba. This limited the Soviets' strategic capabilities in the Western Hemisphere. This standoff at sea reached a very tense point when Soviet ships approached the quarantine line, but they ultimately did not challenge it. This decision likely prevented a direct military confrontation and potential nuclear war.

The resolution of the Cuban missile crisis involved rather intricate diplomatic negotiations. Soviet Premier Nikita Khrushchev offered to remove the missiles in exchange for the US to pledge not to invade Cuba. This agreement also included a secret deal to remove US Jupiter missiles from Turkey.

This incident demonstrated the successful use of naval power to enforce the quarantine without triggering a wider conflict and remains a significant example of military strategy and international diplomacy working hand in hand in order to avert a global nuclear disaster.

Soviet-American Naval Confrontations and Espionage

The engagements at sea during the Cold War were not only about displays of naval power but also involved intricate operations of surveillance, intelligence gathering, and technological warfare.

The Cold War era saw numerous naval standoffs. Naval encounters at this time often involved shadowing and aggressive maneuvering. Both the US and Soviet navies engaged in complex games of cat and mouse. These engagements demonstrated their military capabilities and also their readiness to engage in direct conflict if necessary.

Naval espionage was another critical aspect of the era. Submarines and surface ships from both sides frequently were tasked with electronic surveillance and signal intelligence. These operations were aimed at intercepting communications and gathering crucial intelligence on the naval capabilities and strategic positions of their opponents. This intelligence gathering was important. It influenced decisions on naval deployments and the development of counter strategies.

This eventually led to the signing of the Incidents at Sea Agreement in 1972. This agreement prevented accidental conflicts and managed confrontations at sea. By establishing new communication protocols and conduct guidelines, this agreement helped mitigate the risks of misunderstandings or accidental engagements that could escalate into open conflict. Both sides agreed to avoid provocative actions near each other's ships or aircraft, which included clear signaling of intentions. The agreement also created a system to report and resolve any incidents that did occur.

Advances in Missile Technology and Electronic Warfare

The evolution of ship-based missile systems has been a cornerstone in modern naval warfare. These new systems enhance the offensive and defensive capabilities of naval fleets globally. The introduction of the Aegis Combat System is a prime example of this advancement. This system was originally developed by Radio Corporation of America's (RCA) missile and surface radar division, but it is now produced by Lockheed Martin. Aegis is an integrated weapon system that has been adopted by several navies, including the United States, Japan, and Spain. It combines advanced radar and missile systems to provide comprehensive coverage against a wide range of threats from the air, surface, and subsurface.

There was also the development of other systems and weapons like Tomahawk cruise missiles, which have been a mainstay in naval operations since their effective deployment in the 1991 Gulf War, but we will discuss this further in the next chapter.

Satellites and electronic surveillance have revolutionized naval strategy. They extend the reach of naval forces and enhance their ability to monitor, communicate, and respond to threats. The use of satellites enables constant surveillance and real-time data collection over vast oceanic areas. This allows for better strategic positioning and decision-making.

Electronic warfare has also been significant, particularly with the integration of digital technologies. Adaptive electronic warfare uses machine learning to analyze and respond to threats, which improves the effectiveness of naval operations. Techniques like digital radio frequency memory allow for the manipulation of radar signals to create false targets, which enhances naval forces' deception capabilities.

The US Naval Research Laboratory has been at the forefront of developing technologies for electronic warfare, focusing on areas such as quantum information science, neuromorphic computing, and advanced radio frequency devices. Their work continues to push the boundaries of what is possible in electronic and cyber warfare.

Chapter 10 – Modern Naval Conflicts and Technologies

After the Cold War, the geopolitical landscape became more challenging. This era saw an emphasis on coalition building and the creation of joint forces, which was exemplified by the establishment of the NATO Joint Force Command in Norfolk and the recommissioning of the US Second Fleet to enhance Atlantic operations. Strategies shifted toward addressing regional security challenges in specific geographic areas like the Black Sea, Arctic, and Mediterranean regions.

The US Navy and Marine Corps started focusing on understanding the motivations of their adversaries, which allowed them to effectively communicate their military capabilities to deter aggression before it started. The strategy was to maintain peace. Their stance involved careful evaluation of threats and potential consequences for US interests.

After the Cold War, naval strategies relied more on flexibility and technological advancements to promote international collaboration. The focus was placed on addressing global security challenges instead of all-out war. Broader changes in military doctrine involve moving from continental engagements to something more complex involving multi-theater operations that require coordinated responses across different naval platforms and allied forces.

Naval Operations and the Gulf War

During the Gulf War (1990-1991), the deployment of precision-guided munitions marked a significant advancement in naval warfare. Technology allowed these munitions, which included cruise missiles like the Tomahawk, to play a crucial role in the conflict, as they allowed for precise strikes with reduced collateral damage.

Tomahawk missiles were launched from both submarines and surface ships. Submarines became the preferred platform for these strikes due to their stealth capabilities, which allowed them to operate covertly near enemy shores without exacerbating tensions or even revealing their positions.

The Gulf War also highlighted challenges and innovations in mine warfare. The US Navy had to learn how to deal with extensive Iraqi minefields in the Kuwaiti theater of operations. Traditional mine hunting was slow and resource-intensive. This prompted a shift to quicker mine reconnaissance methods. They wanted to identify mine areas quickly, as it would allow for safer navigation and planning of amphibious assaults. While attempts were made, the effectiveness of this strategy was mixed. US vessels were still damaged on a regular basis by mines.

Naval Encounters of the Gulf War

Battle of Bubiyan

Also known as the Bubiyan Turkey Shoot, the Battle of Bubiyan was a decisive naval engagement that took place from January 29th to February 2nd, 1991. It took place in the waters between Bubiyan Island and the Shatt al-Arab marshlands. The Iraqi Navy attempted to escape to Iran to avoid destruction. However, they were confronted and overwhelmingly defeated by a combined fleet from the United States, the United Kingdom, and Canada.

In this particular battle, British Royal Navy Lynx helicopters were used extensively. They used Sea Skua missiles to devastating effect. These missiles are lightweight, air-launched anti-ship missiles developed by the United Kingdom. They are the opposite of the Sea Dart, which was launched from ships as anti-aircraft missiles. The helicopters were responsible for destroying a significant portion of the Iraqi fleet, sinking fourteen vessels, which included minesweepers, fast attack craft, and patrol boats. Over the course of the entire battle, twenty-one of the twenty-two Iraqi ships attempting to escape were destroyed. The encounter was decidedly one-sided.

An interesting aspect of this battle was the defensive actions taken by the coalition forces. An Iraqi Silkworm missile was launched at the USS *Missouri*. A British destroyer, the HMS *Gloucester*, successfully intercepted it with a Sea Dart missile. This marked the first time a ship-launched anti-air missile intercepted an incoming enemy missile in combat at sea. The coalition forces were not only incredibly coordinated but also had advanced capabilities to support each other.

The Battle of Bubiyan left the Iraqi Navy decimated to the point where it ceased to exist as a functional fighting force and depleted Iraqi maritime capabilities.

The USS *Missouri* and the USS *Wisconsin*

The USS *Missouri* (BB-63) and USS *Wisconsin* (BB-64) were two of America's last battleships. They played a pivotal role in their final combat deployment during the Gulf War. These battleships provided significant naval gunfire support and launched Tomahawk missiles against Iraqi targets. They were a crucial part of the coalition's military strategy.

The USS *Missouri* was also known as "Mighty Mo" and fired its first Tomahawk missile at Baghdad on January 17th, 1991. This particular engagement marked the beginning of its active engagement in Operation Desert Storm. Over the next few days, it launched a total of twenty-eight Tomahawk missiles. The *Missouri* also used traditional naval gunfire, using its massive 16-inch guns to bombard Iraqi artillery positions. This was the first time these guns had been used in combat since the Korean War. This fire support was part of the preparation for a possible amphibious landing, although the actual coalition advance ended up coming across the land border from Saudi Arabia.

The USS *Wisconsin* conducted extensive gunfire missions. The presence of both of these ships in the Gulf War was instrumental in deceiving Iraqi forces into expecting an amphibious assault. This tied up units along the coast instead of inland, where the actual coalition forces were crossing the land borders from Saudi Arabia.

Even though modern warfare increasingly emphasized air power and precision-guided munitions, battleships still had a purpose. Their participation in the Gulf War marked a significant, if not final, chapter in the storied history of battleships in naval warfare.

Iraqi Maritime Embargo

The United Nations Security Council decided to implement a comprehensive maritime embargo against Iraq. This embargo significantly impacted its economy by targeting its oil exports. It was established shortly after Iraq's invasion of Kuwait in August 1990. The UN Security Council Resolution 661 enforced a strict blockade that prevented Iraq from selling oil, which was a major source of its national revenue. Doing this deprived Saddam Hussein's regime of the financial resources it needed to sustain the military operations and governance.

The embargo also restricted most of Iraq's international trade, which contributed to a severe economic decline. This was part of a broader strategy to pressure Iraq into withdrawing from Kuwait and complying with international law.

The embargo was successful. It curtailed Iraq's ability to rebuild its military capabilities and fund its war efforts. A fleet of multinational forces intercepted ships suspected of breaching the embargo. These ships ensured compliance through military and legal means. This naval operation was critical in maintaining the effectiveness of the sanctions placed on Iraq. These sanctions remained largely in place until after Saddam Hussein's regime fell in 2003.

Piracy

Much like the times of the ancient Romans and the ancient Greeks, piracy, especially in the Horn of Africa, poses a significant threat to international shipping. This has prompted extensive international naval cooperation in order to address these security challenges and secure one of the world's busiest shipping lanes.

The European Union Naval Forces Operation Atalanta, launched in December 2008, is a notable effort in fighting piracy. This particular operation has been vital in curbing piracy and protecting vessels of the World Food Programme delivering humanitarian aid to Somalia. They also deter and disrupt piracy and armed robbery at sea. The operation has been effective enough to extend its mandate.

The Combined Task Force 151 is a multinational coalition that has also been instrumental in efforts to fight piracy. Command of this force alternates between various countries, and this task force focuses on deterring, disrupting, and suppressing piracy activities. More specifically, it is there to enhance the security of commercial maritime routes.

The international community's response is not just reactive but also proactive. Naval forces continuously patrol high-risk areas and engage in direct combat with pirate forces whenever necessary. This strong military presence has been complemented by legal and structural reforms in countries most affected by pirates.

Cutting-edge Naval Technology and the Future of Naval Warfare

Warfare has significantly changed, especially when it comes to naval warfare, due to advancements in naval technology. Modern navies have the addition of stealth technology, rail guns, and even laser weapons. New stealth technology reduces radar and infrared signatures, making naval vessels harder to detect and track. This is becoming increasingly important in modern naval strategy because of the emphasis on the element of surprise and reducing enemy engagement opportunities.

Rail guns represent a significant leap in projectile technology. These guns use electromagnetic forces to launch projectiles over long distances and at incredible speeds, and it is done without traditional explosive propellants. Ships can now strike from longer rages while reducing the risks associated with carrying explosives. Japan has notably conducted successful shipboard firing tests of rail guns. Advances are being taken toward practical application in defense against threats like hypersonic missiles.

Laser weapons have been explored for decades, and we are now seeing real-world applications on ships. These weapons often use precision targeting and have the capability to neutralize threats at the speed of light. They are particularly useful against drones and small craft. Laser weapons provide a cost-effective defense mechanism with the potential of unlimited ammunition as it depends only on one's power availability.

The future of naval warfare also strongly leans toward the integration of artificial intelligence (AI) and even unmanned vessels. AI enhances the processing of immense amounts of data to support decision-making and operational efficiency. You can see this in projects like the UK's Defence Science and Technology Laboratory's intelligent ship initiative. This initiative aims to equip the Royal Navy with AI-driven capabilities by 2040.

Unmanned vessels are being designed for both surface and underwater ships and are set to revolutionize naval operations. They will be able to perform various tasks currently handled by manned ships, including reconnaissance, mine countermeasures, and complex attack missions. The advantages are numerous. There is reduced risk to human life, lower costs, and the ability to operate in hazardous environments. The advancements we have made in autonomous technology allow these vessels to perform tasks with increasing independence, and this has been further augmented by AI.

Advancements in technology suggest that naval warfare will have a future where stealth, precision, and unmanned operations will become central elements of naval capabilities and strategy.

Navies in the 21st Century

In the 21st century, global maritime power has witnessed significant shifts. Rapid economic growth in countries like China and India has enabled new nations to use increased resources to expand and modernize their naval capabilities. There is a rise of new naval powers, which brings new challenges to Western powers, particularly the United States, which have traditionally been dominant on the seas. The US has historically leveraged its naval supremacy to influence global affairs and enforce security across key maritime routes.

China's naval expansion is especially notable. The Chinese have developed one of their first overseas military bases in Djibouti, which signals a strategic intent to protect their maritime interests far beyond their regional waters. China seeks to secure its trade routes and assert its presence in international waters. This change in maritime power has prompted the US and its allies to reassess their naval strategies and capabilities in order to properly respond to Beijing's growing maritime assertiveness.

Naval forces will continue to play a role in safeguarding maritime security and making sure that commerce flows freely. Approximately 90 percent of global trade is transported by sea, which makes maritime security critical to global economic stability. The US Navy, among others, performs a variety of roles, including counter-piracy, drug interdiction, and environmental protection in order to collectively help maintain order at sea.

Navies are proving to be an instrumental tool in diplomatic roles as well, which is often referred to as gunboat diplomacy. A naval presence helps to influence the behavior of other states during peacetime. A naval presence can deter potential adversaries, reassure allies, and ensure access to global maritime commerce.

Naval forces are often the first responders to humanitarian crises. They are capable of delivering critical aid and providing logistic support during natural disasters. Essentially, navies reinforce the soft power of maritime nations.

Conclusion

It is pretty clear that naval warfare has undergone dramatic transformations from ancient times. History reflects the ever-evolving dynamics of military technology and geopolitical landscapes. At first, naval confrontations were simple and primarily involved hand-to-hand combat or ramming in battles like those described in the ancient Homeric legends. The advent of the Age of Sail in the 17th century marked a shift to where ships were equipped with new tactics and broadside guns to dominate naval engagements. The Age of Sail emphasizes the strategic importance of wind and formation in naval battles. Maintaining a cohesive line was critical for effective combat.

The introduction of steam-powered ironclads in the 19th century only further revolutionized naval warfare. Strong and heavily armed warships could operate independently of the wind. The Industrial Revolution continued to quickly change people's definition of ships in the 20th century, which witnessed the rise of the aircraft carrier. The aircraft carrier fundamentally altered naval strategies by introducing the concept of airpower working in tandem with ships on the seas. Today, modern naval warfare is characterized by a blend of advanced technology and complex tactics that involve submarines, missiles, and cyber warfare capabilities.

Traditional naval strategies and technological innovations continue to influence modern naval tactics and technologies. The strategic principles of control of the seas and power projection, which were critical during the Age of Sail, remain relevant as modern navies seek to secure and defend maritime trade routes and national borders.

New global security challenges will likely shape the future of naval warfare. There is a rise in irregular warfare tactics, an increase in regional tensions in strategic waterways, and a proliferation of advanced military technologies by state and non-state actors. As navies around the world adapt to these ever-evolving threats, they will likely lean heavily on the development of unmanned systems, artificial intelligence, and advanced cyber warfare capabilities.

New technology allows navies to be more precise, efficient, and safe when engaging the enemy. They reduce the risk to human life and potentially alter the nature of naval engagements. The integration of space-based assets and increased reliance on electronic warfare will redefine strategies and tactics and make information gathering a key element in future naval conflicts.

Naval warfare has shaped and been shaped by technological and strategic innovations throughout history. As global security challenges evolve, naval tactics and technologies will continue to adapt. The lessons from past naval conflicts will undoubtedly inform future strategies, ensuring that naval forces remain a pivotal component of national defense and international security strategy.

If you enjoyed this book, a review on Amazon would be greatly appreciated because it would mean a lot to hear from you.

To leave a review:
1. Open your camera app.
2. Point your mobile device at the QR code.
3. The review page will appear in your web browser.

Thanks for your support!

Here's another book by Captivating History that you might like

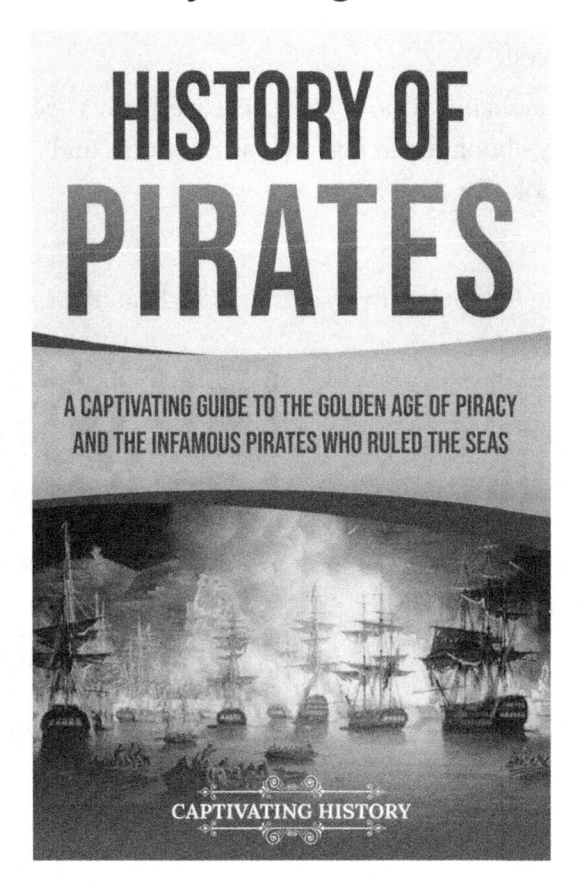

HISTORY OF PIRATES

A CAPTIVATING GUIDE TO THE GOLDEN AGE OF PIRACY AND THE INFAMOUS PIRATES WHO RULED THE SEAS

CAPTIVATING HISTORY

Free Bonus from Captivating History (Available for a Limited time)

Hi History Lovers!

Now you have a chance to join our exclusive history list so you can get your first history ebook for free as well as discounts and a potential to get more history books for free!

Simply visit the link below to join.

Or, Scan the QR code!

captivatinghistory.com/ebook

Also, make sure to follow us on Facebook, X, and YouTube by searching for Captivating History.

References

Chapter 1

"Early Seafaring: Beyond the Blue Horizon" https://www.world-archaeology.com/features/early-seafaring-beyond-the-blue-horizon/ Accessed: April 9, 2024.

"The Ancient Egyptian Navy" https://worldhistory.us/ancient-history/ancient-egypt/the-ancient-egyptian-navy.php Accessed: April 9, 2024.

Shaw, Ian (1999). *Egyptian Warfare and Weapons*. Shire Publications.

"Ancient European Wayfinders: The Minoans Who Sailed By the Stars" https://popular-archaeology.com/article/ancient-european-wayfinders-the-minoans-who-sailed-by-the-stars/ Accessed: April 9, 2024.

"Minoan Ship Construction" https://www.minoanatlantis.com/Minoan_Shipbuilding.php Accessed: April 9, 2024.

"Phoenician Ships" https://exploration.marinersmuseum.org/watercraft/phoenician-ships/ Accessed: April 9, 2024.

Chapter 2

"Themistocles: Champion of Athenian Sea Power" https://www.usni.org/magazines/naval-history-magazine/2022/april/themistocles-champion-athenian-sea-power Accessed: April 11, 2024.

"Themistocles: The Father of Naval Warfare" https://cimsec.org/themistocles-father-naval-warfare/ Accessed: April 11, 2024.

"The Greek Trireme" https://warfarehistorynetwork.com/the-greek-trireme/ Accessed: April 11, 2024.

"Battle of Salamis: The Unexpected Greek Victory over the Persians" https://www.thecollector.com/battle-of-salamis/ Accessed: April 11, 2024.

"Battle of Artemisium: The Greek Fleet vs The Persian Empire" https://www.thecollector.com/battle-of-artemisium/ Accessed: April 11, 2024.

"Battle of Mycale: The Last Battle of the Greco-Persian War" https://www.thecollector.com/battle-of-mycale/ Accessed: April 11, 2024.

"Battle of the Eurymedon" http://www.thelatinlibrary.com/historians/notes/eurymedon.html Accessed: April 11, 2024.

"Learn About the Battle of Aegospotami" https://www.greekboston.com/culture/ancient-history/battle-aegospotami/ Accessed: April 11, 2024.

Chapter 3

"Rome at Sea: The Beginnings of Roman Naval Power" https://www.cambridge.org/core/journals/greece-and-rome/article/rome-at-sea-the-beginnings-of-roman-naval-power/F7E12E81A2E03D4C3F032CB82F335C5F Accessed: April 13, 2024.

"Aiding the Ascendancy of the Roman Navy" https://www.usni.org/magazines/naval-history-magazine/2016/august/aiding-ascendancy-roman-navy Accessed: April 13, 2024.

"The First Punic War: Audacity and Hubris" https://www.usni.org/magazines/naval-history-magazine/2021/august/first-punic-war-audacity-and-hubris Accessed: April 13, 2024.

"Battle of Aegates" https://imperiumromanum.pl/en/battles/battle-of-aegates/ Accessed: April 13, 2024.

"Ecnomus" https://www.livius.org/articles/battle/ecnomus-256-bce/ Accessed: April 13, 2024.

"Battle of Drepana" https://history-maps.com/story/First-Punic-War/event/Battle-of-Drepana Accessed: April 13, 2024.

"Cilician Pirates" https://www.livius.org/articles/people/cilician-pirates/ Accessed: April 13, 2024.

"Ancient Rome and the Pirates" https://www.historytoday.com/archive/ancient-rome-and-pirates Accessed: April 13, 2024.

"Pompey and the Pirates" https://www.romanhistoria.com/2019/11/pompey-and-pirates.html Accessed: April 13, 2024.

"The Roman Navy: When Rome Ruled the Sea" https://www.thecollector.com/roman-navy/ Accessed: April 13, 2024.

"Roman Navy" https://roman-empire.net/army/fleet/ Accessed: April 13, 2024.

"Battle of Actium" https://www.worldhistory.org/Battle_of_Actium/ Accessed: April 13, 2024.

Chapter 4

"Crafting the Past: How Were Viking Longships Constructed?" https://ancientpedia.com/how-were-viking-longships-constructed/ Accessed: April 15, 2024.

"Making a Viking Ship" https://regia.org/research/ships/Ships1.htm Accessed: April 15, 2024.

"Viking expeditions and raids" https://en.natmus.dk/historical-knowledge/denmark/prehistoric-period-until-1050-ad/the-viking-age/expeditions-and-raids/ Accessed: April 15, 2024.

"Vikings" https://www.history.com/topics/exploration/vikings-history Accessed: April 15, 2024.

"The Viking Riad on Lindisfarne" https://www.english-heritage.org.uk/visit/places/lindisfarne-priory/History/viking-raid/ Accessed: April 15, 2024.

"Vikings Attack Lindisfarne" https://www.historytoday.com/archive/months-past/vikings-attack-lindisfarne Accessed: April 15, 2024.

"The Siege of Paris" https://historymedieval.com/the-siege-of-paris-city-under-fire/ Accessed: April 15, 2024.

"What happened when the Vikings Raided Seville?" https://www.thevikingherald.com/article/what-happened-when-the-vikings-raided-seville/305 Accessed: April 15, 2024.

Chapter 5

"1492: An Ongoing Voyage" https://www.loc.gov/exhibits/1492/columbus.html Accessed: April 17, 2024.

"Vasco da Gama reaches India" https://www.history.com/this-day-in-history/vasco-da-gama-reaches-india Accessed: April 17, 2024.

"The Portuguese Conquest of India" https://www.worldhistory.org/article/2025/the-portuguese-conquest-of-india/ Accessed: April 17, 2024.

"Ferdinand Magellan" https://www.history.com/topics/exploration/ferdinand-magellan Accessed: April 17, 2024,

"Ferdinand Magellan" https://www.worldhistory.org/Ferdinand_Magellan/ Accessed: April 17, 2024.

"Lessons of Strategy from the Battle of Mactan" https://fmapulse.com/fma-corner/fma-corner-lessons-strategy-battle-mactan/ Accessed: April 17, 2024.

"Searching for the Northwest Passage" https://www.rmg.co.uk/stories/topics/search-northwest-passage Accessed: April 17, 2024.

"Henry Hudson" https://www.history.com/topics/exploration/henry-hudson Accessed: April 17, 2024.

"Landing of Henrick Hudson, 1609" https://www.gilderlehrman.org/history-resources/spotlight-primary-source/landing-henrick-hudson-1609 Accessed: April 17, 2024.

"Franklin Expedition: A Story of Loss and Rediscovery" https://www.historicmysteries.com/history/the-doomed-franklin-expedition/825/ Accessed: April 17, 2024.

"What Happened to the Doomed Franklin Expedition? These Are the Clues" https://www.history.com/news/franklin-expedition-mystery-northwest-passage Accessed: April 17, 2024.

Chapter 6

"Ships of the Line" https://navalmechanicsofthebattleofdominica.omeka.net/exhibits/show/naval-tactics/ships-of-the-line Accessed: April 19, 2024.

"The battle of the Gabbard, 2 June 1653" https://www.rmg.co.uk/collections/objects/rmgc-object-11768 Accessed: April 19, 2024.

"The Four Days' Battle: A Dutch Triumph" https://warfarehistorynetwork.com/article/the-four-days-battle-a-dutch-triumph/ Accessed: April 19, 2024.

"Four Days in 1666" https://www.usni.org/magazines/naval-history-magazine/2021/june/four-days-1666 Accessed: April 19, 2024.

"The Trafalgar of the Seven Years' War" https://www.usni.org/magazines/naval-history-magazine/2020/june/trafalgar-seven-years-war Accessed: April 19, 2024.

"The Battle of Quiberon Bay, 20 November 1759" https://www.rmg.co.uk/collections/objects/rmgc-object-11891 Accessed: April 19, 2024.

"The Battle of Trafalgar" https://navalhistoria.com/trafalgar/ Accessed: April 19, 2024.

"The Battle of Trafalgar: The greatest sea battle of the Napoleonic Wars" https://www.historyskills.com/classroom/modern-history/battle-of-trafalgar/ Accessed: April 19, 2024.

"How Did Lord Nelson Win the Battle of Trafalgar So Convincingly?" https://www.historyhit.com/battle-of-trafalgar-victory/ Accessed: April 19, 2024.

Chapter 7

"Ironclads to Dreadnoughts: The Changing Face of Naval Warfare" https://navalhistoria.com/naval/ Accessed: April 21, 2024.

"The advancement in naval technology which influenced the outcome of the American Civil War" https://www.britannica.com/video/195087/advances-technology-armament-propulsion-conduct-outcome-American Accessed: April 21, 2024.

"The Glorie and Warrior" https://www.usni.org/magazines/naval-history-magazine/2022/august/glorie-and-warrior Accessed: April 21, 2024.

"Battle of Hampton Roads" https://www.history.com/topics/american-civil-war/battle-of-hampton-roads Accessed: April 21, 2024.

"Battle of Hampton Roads" https://totallyhistory.com/battle-of-hampton-roads/ Accessed: April 21, 2024.

"Hampton Roads: Monitor vs Merrimack" https://www.battlefields.org/learn/civil-war/battles/hampton-roads Accessed: April 21, 2024.

"Ironclad Clash at Lissa" https://warfarehistorynetwork.com/article/ironclad-clash-at-lissa/ Accessed: April 21, 2024.

"The Battle of Lissa 1866" https://naval-encyclopedia.com/industrial-era/the-battle-of-lissa-1866.php Accessed: April 21, 2024.

"Evolution of the Submarine" https://warfarehistorynetwork.com/article/evolution-of-the-submarine/ Accessed: April 21, 2024.

"The Confederate Ironclad Navy" https://www.usni.org/magazines/naval-history-magazine/2014/january/confederate-ironclad-navy Accessed: April 21, 2024.

"The US Navy and the Naval Battles of Charleston, 1863" https://www.clevelandcivilwarroundtable.com/the-u-s-navy-and-the-naval-battles-of-charleston-1863/ Accessed: April 21, 2024.

"New Navy, New Power" https://www.usni.org/magazines/naval-history-magazine/2013/january/new-navy-new-power Accessed: April 21, 2024.

"The Civil War and Revolutions in Naval Affairs: Lessons for Today" https://ndupress.ndu.edu/Media/News/News-Article-View/Article/3156619/the-civil-war-and-revolutions-in-naval-affairs-lessons-for-today/ Accessed: April 21, 2024.

Chapter 8

"Fighting the Great War at Sea: Strategy, Tactics, and Technology" https://navyhistory.org/2020/08/fighting-the-great-war-at-sea-strategy-tactics/ Accessed: April 23, 2024.

"Naval Warfare: 1914-1918" https://encyclopedia.1914-1918-online.net/article/naval_warfare Accessed: April 23, 2024.

"Warfare Under the Waves – Submarines in the First World War" https://www.warhistoryonline.com/world-war-i/submarines-first-world-war.html Accessed: April 23, 2024.

"U-Boat War in World War One" https://uboat.net/wwi/ Accessed: April 23, 2024.

"Unrestricted U-boat Warfare" https://www.theworldwar.org/learn/about-wwi/unrestricted-u-boat-warfare Accessed: April 23, 2024.

"The Q-Ship – Cause and Effect" https://www.usni.org/magazines/proceedings/1953/may/q-ship-cause-and-effect Accessed: April 23, 2024.

"Britain's WWI Mystery Q-Ships" https://www.historic-uk.com/HistoryUK/HistoryofBritain/Mystery-Ships/ Accessed: April 23, 2024.

"Battle of Heligoland Bight" https://www.britishbattles.com/first-world-war/the-battle-of-heligoland-bight/ Accessed: April 23, 2024.

"Battle of Dogger Bank" https://www.britannica.com/event/Battle-of-Dogger-Bank-1915 Accessed: April 23, 2024.

"Battle of Coronel" https://www.britishbattles.com/first-world-war/battle-of-coronel/ Accessed: April 23. 2024.

"Battle of the Falklands" https://encyclopedia.1914-1918-online.net/article/falklands_battle_of_the Accessed: April 23, 2024.

"The Washington Naval Treaty – A Pivotal Moment in Naval Arms Control" https://navalhistoria.com/the-washington-naval-treaty/ Accessed: April 23, 2024.

"Pearl Harbor" https://www.history.com/topics/world-war-ii/pearl-harbor Accessed: April 23, 2024.

"Battle of Midway" https://www.history.com/topics/world-war-ii/battle-of-midway Accessed: April 23, 2024.

"The Battle of Midway" https://www.military-history.org/cover-feature/the-battle-of-midway.htm Accessed: April 23. 2024.

"The Codebreakers' War in the Atlantic" https://warfarehistorynetwork.com/the-codebreakers-war-in-the-atlantic/ Accessed: April 23, 2024.

"The Battle That Had to Be Won" https://www.usni.org/magazines/naval-history-magazine/2008/june/battle-had-be-won Accessed: April 23, 2024.

"Longest Campaign: Winston Churchill and the Atlantic Battle, 1940-43" https://winstonchurchill.hillsdale.edu/bell-atlantic-battle/ Accessed: April 23, 2024.

"Black May 1943" https://www.nationalww2museum.org/about-us/notes-museum/ask-curator-black-may-1943 Accessed: April 23, 2024.

"Great Story: When British Commandos Turned Pirate – Operation Postmaster" https://www.warhistoryonline.com/instant-articles/when-british-commandos-pirate.html Accessed: April 23, 2024.

"Operation Postmaster: The Great Gamble" https://spotterup.com/operation-postmaster-the-great-gamble/ Accessed: April 23, 2024.

Chapter 9

"USS Nautilus (SSN-571)" https://ethw.org/USS_Nautilus_(SSN-571) Accessed: April 25, 2024.

"How the USS Nautilus Forever Transformed U.S. Submarines" https://nationalinterest.org/blog/reboot/how-uss-nautilus-forever-transformed-us-submarines-168666 Accessed: April 25, 2024.

"Submarines in the Cold War" https://americanhistory.si.edu/subs/work/missions/deterrence/index.html Accessed: April 25, 2024.

"The Global Nuclear Balance: Nuclear Forces and Key Trends in Nuclear Modernization" https://www.csis.org/analysis/global-nuclear-balance-nuclear-forces-and-key-trends-nuclear-modernization Accessed: April 25, 2024.

"Cuban Missile Crisis" https://www.history.com/topics/cold-war/cuban-missile-crisis Accessed: April 25, 2024.

"The Cuban Missile Crisis Quarantine" https://www.usni.org/magazines/naval-history-magazine/1991/april/cuban-missile-crisis-quarantine Accessed: April 25, 2024.

"Conflict and Cooperation: The US and Soviet Navies in the Cold War" https://www.history.navy.mil/research/library/online-reading-room/title-list-alphabetically/c/conflict-coop-us-soviet-navies-cold-war.html Accessed: April 25, 2024.

"Cooperation amidst Great Power Rivalry: The United States, the Soviet Union, and the Cold War" https://www.csis.org/analysis/cooperation-amidst-great-power-rivalry-united-states-soviet-union-and-cold-war Accessed: April 25, 2024.

Chapter 10

"Significance of Post-Cold War Deterrence Concepts for the US Navy and Marine Corps" https://nap.nationalacademies.org/read/5464/chapter/5 Accessed: April 27, 2024.

"NATO's Maritime Vigilance: Optimizing the Standing Naval Force for the Future" https://warontherocks.com/2022/12/natos-maritime-vigilance-optimizing-the-standing-naval-force-for-the-future/ Accessed: April 27, 2024.

"Gulf War: Naval Lessons of the Gulf War" https://www.defensemedianetwork.com/stories/gulf-war-naval-lessons-of-the-gulf-war/ Accessed: April 27, 2024.

"That time the US and its allies destroyed the entire Iraqi Navy" https://www.wearethemighty.com/mighty-trending/us-navy-gulf-war/ Accessed: April 27, 2024.

"Annihilation of the Iraqi Navy" https://history-maps.com/story/Gulf-War/event/Annihilation-of-the-Iraqi-Navy Accessed: April 27, 2024.

"Why 50-Year-Old Battleships Were a Critical Part of Operation Desert Storm" https://www.military.com/history/why-50-year-old-battleships-were-critical-part-of-operation-desert-storm.html Accessed: April 27, 2024.

"The Gulf War (1990-1991)" https://ussmissouri.org/learn-the-history/operation-desert-storm/ Accessed: April 27, 2024.

"Iraq's Invasion of Kuwait & Gulf War (1990-1991)" https://fanack.com/iraq/history-of-iraq/iraqs-invasion-of-kuwait-and-gulf-war/ Accessed: April 27, 2024.

"Tackling piracy: EU's role crucial for maritime security in the Horn of Africa" https://www.eeas.europa.eu/node/60439_en Accessed: April 27, 2024.

"Piracy is Back in the Horn of Africa – What's Behind its Return?" https://www.rusi.org/explore-our-research/publications/commentary/piracy-back-horn-africa-whats-behind-its-return Accessed: April 27, 2024.

"Japan Performs First Ever Railgun Test From Ship At Sea" https://www.navalnews.com/naval-news/2023/10/japan-performs-first-ever-railgun-test-from-ship-at-sea/ Accessed: April 27, 2024.

"China's Top Navy Scientists Designs Nuclear Aircraft Carrier With Railguns and Lasers" https://www.nextbigfuture.com/2023/09/chinas-top-navy-scientist-designs-nuclear-aircraft-carrier-with-railguns-and-lasers.html Accessed: April 27, 2024.

"Dstl's Intelligent Ship and the future of the Royal Navy" https://www.naval-technology.com/features/dstls-intelligent-ship-and-the-future-of-the-royal-navy/ Accessed: April 27, 2024.

"Modern Naval Warfare: Ships of the Future" https://searchinghero.com/blog/modern-naval-warfare-ships-future/ Accessed: April 27, 2024.

"Sea Power: The US Navy and Foreign Policy" https://www.cfr.org/backgrounder/sea-power-us-navy-and-foreign-policy Accessed: April 27, 2024.

"A Maritime Strategy to Deal with China" https://www.usni.org/magazines/proceedings/2022/february/maritime-strategy-deal-china Accessed: April 27, 2024.

"US Naval Power in the 21ˢᵗ Century" https://www.usni.org/press/books/us-naval-power-21st-century Accessed: April 27, 2024.

"The Naval Alliance: Preparing NATO for a maritime century" https://www.atlanticcouncil.org/in-depth-research-reports/report/the-naval-alliance-preparing-nato-for-a-maritime-century/ Accessed: April 27, 2024.

Image Sources

[i] *Cc-by-sa-3.0-fr, CC BY-SA 2.0 FR <https://creativecommons.org/licenses/by-sa/2.0/fr/deed.en>, via Wikimedia Commons; https://commons.wikimedia.org/wiki/File:Gebel_el-Arak_knife_(front_and_back).jpg*

[ii] *https://commons.wikimedia.org/wiki/File:Trireme.jpg*

[iii] *https://commons.wikimedia.org/wiki/File:Corvus_%C3%A4nterbrygga.png*

[iv] *Steen Weile, Notmark, Denmark., CC BY 3.0 <https://creativecommons.org/licenses/by/3.0>, via Wikimedia Commons; https://commons.wikimedia.org/wiki/File:Sebbe_Als_2.jpg*

[v] *https://commons.wikimedia.org/wiki/File:Vaisseau_fran%C3%A7ais_le_Saint-Esprit_au_combat_en_1782.jpg*

[vi] *File:U995 2001 1.jpg: Darkone (talk · contribs) derivative work: Georgfotoart, CC BY-SA 2.0 <https://creativecommons.org/licenses/by-sa/2.0>, via Wikimedia Commons; https://commons.wikimedia.org/wiki/File:U995_2001_1_b.jpg*

[vii] *https://commons.wikimedia.org/wiki/File:HMS_Dreadnought_1906_H61017.jpg*

Made in United States
North Haven, CT
07 May 2025

68668265R00065